POLLUTION TO PURITY OF ENVIRONMENT

POLLUTION TO PURITY OF ENVIRONMENT

GURCHARAN SINGH

DEEP & DEEP PUBLICATIONS PVT. LTD.
F-159, Rajouri Garden, New Delhi-110027

ISBN 81-7629-236-2

Typeset by ASHISH TECHNOGRAPHICS,
3190, Mohindra Park, Shakur Basti, Delhi-110034.

Printed in India at EFFICIENT OFFSET PRINTERS,
Plot-215, Industrial Area, Shahzada Bagh, Delhi.

Published by DEEP & DEEP PUBLICATIONS PVT. LTD.
F-159, Rajouri Garden, New Delhi-110027.
Phones : 5435369, 5440916

CONTENTS

PREFACE

This writing is my humble endeavour to record my impressions and imprints, which my mind has assimilated into my mental constitution. These imprints have been carved out in retrospect and their projections have been gauged in prospective graphics.

Actually it is the language of the mind only, which leads the faculties of a person to actualism. All the makes and breaks, good or bad, greed and avarice, care and compassions, are the creations of the mind, itself it is the mind only, which attracts a person to purity or pollution. The only difference being is, as to whether the mind is kept in subjugation to wisdom or is subjugated to sensual desires. The latter being a short cut to worldly comforts. The general tendency has taken the centre stage to seek happiness and enjoyments, in the perpetualism of worldly pursuits only.

No dividing line, is observed between achieving these ends, through divine paths and ill conceived selfish greed, which has put the humanity in disarray and disharmony. That is why the society is going toward decomposition and degeneration. The Indian culture was impregnated in divinity, and all its practices were according to the divine perceptions. But, the times have changed and the cultural gap of different cultures over this planet have squeezed to such an extent that no culture can now be stamped as alien or separate.

This syndrome of short cuts has penetrated deep into our system and no section is now spared to stick to our original tenets. Rather 95% of the people are observing a hi-fi dictums in their general behavior. The politicians, the helms men, officialdom, priest hood, all have been poisoned by the sting of avarice and greed. Which has polluted our society to incorrigible limits.

Through this writing I have tried to observe our basic tenets in the pattern of "then and now".

I may be permitted to say that I am not a man of words, kindly ignore my mistakes and do take the trouble to follow the essence of this text. There would be so many words which might have been mis-spelled or wrongly adjusted, for which I would extend my humble regrets.

I am grateful to my daughter Dr. Kulbir Kaur, Lecturer in English literature at Chandigarh, who always encourages me to keep up.

Also my most grateful thanks, I extend to Miss Amandeep Kaur, who helped me in correcting and reprinting the manuscript.

Mohali GURCHARAN SINGH

1

DYNAMICS OF HUMAN MIND

Deep carvings and curvatures, in the cerebral structure of human brain, have created such complexities, that the man equipped with even the deepest conceptual esteem, himself is lost thin. The material existence, which can be evaluated through the time, space and causal dimensions, in the deep seas of infiniteness, are only a terra-firma in the limitless evolutions and dissolutions going on in the universe.

The objective knowledge, which has uptill now been discovered by the man through scientific adventures is only said to be a limited one. Our visionaries have given us in our religious books, that the knowledge measurable by the dimensional parameters, can be transferred and passed on from one generation to the other. Even its factual results can be verified and changed by the future scientists, but the subjective knowledge is not transferable and hence remains the prized possession of the vision and insight.

From the times immemorial, our seers, the masters of subjectivity, could only guide their disciples to achieve it, through yoga. Its ultimate goal was the knowledge of self, through control of one's mind. That is, "Conquest of the mind, is the conquest of the world".—*Guru Nanak*.

This is the end of man's journey, and the salvation of his soul also.

There should be no clash between the objective and subjective researchers, as both are engaged in the discovery of the hidden knowledge. The only difference is, that, the objective knowledge can be gauged for its accuracy, and realism, in the three parameters of existence. That is why it becomes congruent with the normal intelligence and can be synchronised with the rational thought of the people from time to time. It is a major input of 'cause and effect' complexes of material world, and is a mother of all, pride and prejudice, war and peace, inventions and innovations etc. It also clarifies the superstitious mystification of mind, and thus makes the civic life of people, more transparent and promotes a civilized social order.

The reverse side of this knowledge, is that it catalysis the human mind to securing of more and more material wealth, by states who rule supreme in the accumulation of this knowledge and thus promotes the cult of slavery and subjugation of the weak nations. The powerful nations start looking to procure the scientists and technologists of the weak countries, to get their own, defensive and offensive, import and export, commerce and trade, paraphirnelia sharpened, to make their own arsenals, hawkish and awesome for the weaker nations. Thus it can be said that this knowledge of objectivity makes itself, a commercial and salable commodity in the sensual metaphysics of the world mind set.

The subjective knowledge is the acquisition of the knowledge of the inner recesses of the human consciousness, and can be achieved only by the complex processes of sublimation exercised by our seers and visionaries, through complete controls and commands of their senses, by provoking their intelligence. Their cerebral arsenal would work to the well-fare and well being of not only the human beings but also of all beings. They work as per the divine reflection of their mind, which cannot be put as a sale and purchase commodity. This knowledge is stated to be an instrument of perfect Bliss and it cannot be gauged or transferred. These people are called as Satpurshas, the apostles of truth and peace, the knowers, the seers and are the great pivots of our religious philosophy. Their lives become a pointer to morality, simplicity, renunciations, and they may guide their followers to achieve this knowledge, but it cannot be transferred or sold and hence cannot become a commercial commodity.

The general human mind remains under the influence of illusion of material gains only, as the worldly chess is chequered in short cuts to achieve comforts and cosyness of routine life pattern. Only the acquisition of more and more money, power and pelf, status and titles, are the choicest-aptitudinal channels, which guide the human mind to tread on. As the saying goes on, that money makes the mare go, hence the money takes the driving seat in the dynamics of man's intellectual contours. May there be some tangential touches for religious rituals here and there to identify oneself in consonance with certain creed, but the main thrust of the man's activism remains with the worldly gains only. We daily find people, in politics or bureaucracy, attempting to get themselves slotted in respectful social status, where in he may get a potential position, to share the commands and controls of the official worthiness.

There are mostly the parasitic deviations in the routine of these people, who are more hypocrite than real. So what! it is the order of the day. This is how the mind of the general human being is working.

2

ESSENTIALS OF EXISTENCE

From the times immemorial, our seers and guides, have made our society believe that the man only needs three basic things to tread on the path of human-graphics in ones life. They had been also guiding us to observe penance and perseverance in all spheres of our activities.

The three basics, they had enumerated as "Home, Hearth and Helmet. No doubt all these three, are subject to their maintenance, through money and money only. For the achievement of this motive, they had also given us a set pattern of human endeavors, fixed, in certain parameters, and had advised the human race not to contravene those parameters, otherwise the man would suffer from the mental as well as physical disorders.

Now with the passage of time, the old perceptions have been rendered totally redundant by the man-made short-cuts and selfish tendencies, and a sort of rat-race is going on, on all sides of the world, in which the only object of life seems to be collection of money. With the new innovations, the new trade laws have come up in national and international arena and to opt these practices has, (to some extent) become a necessity. The moral content of our culture and traditions has now taken a back seat, and the driving force is the unethical and unprincipled tendencies, which are sprouting and multiplying everyday, in these fast changing conditions.

Whatever laws, in the global scenario, we are confronting right now, we can stick to our moral values, as some of our leaders had shown us but the majority of our people have flown with the tidal waves of the times, and under the tempting and crazy shortcuts, for collecting money to lead luxurious lives, live in palatial buildings, and acquire immovable properties, have gone to the hilt, in deceiving their own people, and make a mockery of the law of the land. By opting to such practices, they have opened up so many complicated and allied channels to conceal it, and also through a self deceipt hint to others, to follow their foot prints, and hence this rat race has set in. No doubt the hands of the law of the land are still sustainable and the saner elements in our legislatures and parliament are alive to such contingencies but the forces which have laundered money with unethical means, try to put the cart before the horse, to get themselves prove before the law, that actually they are innocent. If their cynicism can be reoriented with the helmsmen in real politick, they refound and refurbish their image in the people and emerge with new reflexes, to gain political as well as social, eulogisation.

This sort of flexibility in laws, which can be exploited and twisted in favour of the culprit make the germs of unethical flows, grow in the social spectrum of all nations.

The original doctrinal perceptions, which I have discussed in the beginning naturally pale down, and its essence is lost thin, in the minds of the general population. The people become habitual to see their material lives easy and smooth. There are (only a few) who follow their esteems or consciousness.

Only leave aside our seers, as Guru Nanak, Bhagat Kabir, Bhagat Ravidas and many more of the likes, who attained a status of absolute consciousness, while the people in general are the worshippers of Lakhshami only, as even the Shivji Bhagwan, the apostle of knowledge, was driven out by a millionaire's wife, when Lakhshami (under a compromised contest with Shivji), requested the wife of the millionaire, to, "drive this Avdhoot out, if she wanted her (Lakhshami) to stay at her house".

My people still perform Lakhshami Puja on the day of

Deepawali. Anyway no body on the earth these days, would say "no" to the money and material. However I would say that he who is content, with his honest means is taken as a wise and contented one, and would leave this body frame without any tension. This is how our thinkers evaluate this subject.

The three essentials of existence, is not only the need of the man, even the lives other than the humans, do also need it. The reptile, birds, parasite and animal life also need it. But the nature has ordained them so, that they have their progenics they have their homes in the forms of nests or dens and they also yearn and feed their new borns. The nature has made their outer structures so, that they could protect their bodies from the vagaries of the season. The nature is so benevolent to them that they never take to the contravention of its laws.

The human mind which is destined to use its faculties, to incorporate its commands and controls in coordination with its intellectual apparatus, is the main culprit to contravene them, simply to satisfy his own ego. The point in case is, the food habits of all the animals are fixed by nature and no animal ever contravenes it. The horse, cow, elephant always take vegetarian food where as lion, cats etc. are fixed for non-veg. So these animals would only accept their foods, which nature has fixed for them. Only the man is defying the nature, because of the satisfaction of his silvary taste.

The wisdom compels, to analyse as to what the needs of a man are. Is there any relationship between a glutton and a hungry man? Hunger can be satisfied but the temptation of eyes can not. It has been seen that some people display the show of their being rich, to the limits of criminality, and it appears that the spirit of the toiling people is being trumpetted under feet. Such type of criminal waste of wealth leaves certain under currents and they set the spirits of righteousness and rationalism, revolt against the system and social laws as Sahir Ludhianavi, has said while visiting the Taj Mahal at Agra:

"Kissi shah Ne Lekar Aapni Daulat Ka Sahara

Hum Griboon Ki Mahabat Ka Orai Hai Mazak"

that is (a king has played a joke with the love-born attributes of the poor, taking advantage of his wealth).

So the sensuous temptations does not come under the ambit of essentials of life, rather it becomes a specific deterrent in promoting the good relationship amongst the people. I had the opportunity to hear from some money minded people that they want to leave so much after their death that their seven generations would enjoy their living without doing any effort to earn. What a foul and frivolous idea ? It appears, that they want to have a crippled and effortless descendants.

One should not leave any thing behind except the talented and an asset-prone members, in the oceans of societical plane. An idle person remains a burden on society and would not even remain in his normal self. Such sensuous temptations on the part of old generation are also not appreciable. In some families, the old people are found more inclined towards the material wealth. They incorporate their experiences to advise their younger one's, to have all sorts of scandalous and leacherous, invectitudes of mind applied, to collect the material wealth. They don't even hesitate to harm the interest of some others. They are non-believers of sins, being conducted in contrast to the voice of their consciousness. Actually such men cannot give even blessings to the person, who may touch their feet, which people believe in, as the voice of God, as it is presumed that in the matured age, the person does penance for all his misdeeds in the life and prays for pardon from God. The waves ushered in by the consciousness of an old man, are presumed to create an aura, which purifies every being, who comes in its ambit. But there are some souls whose temperament is so inclined towards the lower end of their mind, that their thought syndromes, never touche the graphics of divine parameters.

It is therefore my humble submission that the men in matured stage of their age, must adopt a conduct, which behove of them. The general presumption is that the wisdom level of the old person, attained through the summation of his experiences in life, has touched such levels that it is valued in the domain of divinity now, and as Baba Farid says:

"Uth Farida Suttyn Teri Dhari Hoi Bhur

Agga Nere Aa. Gia Pichha, Reh Gia Dur"

(Baba Farid prays to God, that now his end is approaching near, let this humble servant of yours, be have your benevolence, to shatter all covers of slumbers, which have covered him with sins and let this humble soul be freed on the day of riddance).

Even giving a definition of old age, a poet of Urdu, (Titled as Addamm) says

"Gunahon Se Jee Ukta Gia Hai Addamm

Shaid Bhuddpa A Gia Hai"

that is (Addamm says, I do not want to lead a sinful life now, it appears I have grown older)

This too is an accepted truth, that a man keeps away from all misdeeds and sins when the shadow of old age, begin covering his body frame. The old people therefore keep their right, to be respected by every body, may be his own nears and dears or some other people. He should not get his respected surname as "Babaji" to be contemptuous in the social encounters in general behaviour pattern. His piece of advice should be humane, and in real sense, he should pray that, "All he blessed". The partisan thought strokes from such people, bring disrespect and disrepute to the stage of silver-lines-days. The twin-light years of even the good, and God fearing souls, also get mystified, as the people find this lacuna, to defame an otherwise respectful slots for this age.

The man must remain with the essential limits for the existence of his family. The acquisition of wealth, by scams, and scandals, would ultimately take our people to mental pollution and the nation as a whole will be put to degradation, for which only the people in authorities would be responsible. It is a fact, in absolutism, that tendencies to give name and fame to money launderers, on political scenario of our country, should be discouraged in all compartments. At least we should not allow such persons to pull the strings, to unfurl the national flag, who so ever it may be. There are already under currents in our people that the battery of sycophants and jugglery of words, on such occasions, make such person enjoy the epithet of leaders or Netajee. As we see now that there is no dearth of leaders these days, while the sewadar is non. We must see reason to discard such crooks, conferred with leadership, by their relatives. Otherwise I fear that the list of essentials for their existence, would not limit to the foreign bank accounts only, but they would now be aspiring for transmission channel for their entertainments in the orbital trajectories of other planets in the family of sun.

With all humiliation, I would request all my right thinking countrymen to see the torn and tethered clothes, of my people who are busy in the day-to-day construction and fascination of our country. Have a sigh when you see a malneutritioned baby sucking the chest of his mother, who hold her, while supporting a container of cement and bajri to strength the foundation of a piller. A rickshaw puller, a scavenger, a tiller, a poor farmers, and million others who come under this category and are below the line of poverty, only these people know the values of the essentials of human existence. It is my submission that if we can stick to our honest means, we would help in raising the level of our country men. But without hesitation I may say that it is not the subject of Hi-Fi-culture who have not seen, hunger, drudgery dungeons, darkness, demolishings, diseases, and dust etc.

3

PERCEPTS AND PRACTICES

My point under discussion is the 'Percepts and practices to manage the worldly affairs, the impediments and inhibitions in their accomplishments and how the man made paraphrinelia. has been a deterrent in the achievement of its goals.

The main actors responsible for re-orientation and reformation of a healthy civilian set up, are:

1. Politician and Helmsmen
2. Bureaucrats and Government servants
3. Preachers and Social reformers
4. Scientists and Technocrats

The minds of all the four categories are sick and polluted, hypocrite and hybrid, mercenary and myopic, drab and detrimental, inactive and invective, in the general frame of our managerial skills. This is the projected opinion of the people in general. This belief has been concretised and has made a permanent slot in the minds of the people, when they daily analyse the activities of these people, on different electronic media channels in programmes, like, "Aap ki Adalat", "Face to face", "Know your city", and rhetorics of Jaspal Bhatti and likes, as flop show etc. alongwith the opinion of the general public as a back drop in the daily news. Also the newspapers and news magazines with which the stalls are overflowing are doing their duties to create an awareness in the people's mind to avoid complacency and be watchful to guard themselves from the onslaughts of irresponsible state activism.

WHY, WHERE AND WHEN

These three interrogative's, are the most complex syndrome in the schemes of developmental plans which are perceived and conceptualised by the planners, for the welfare of the people, under the projected policy declaration of our legislative, but their implementations are subject to the formal cushion clearance of the minister at the helm of the affairs, till that time, these beautifully bound, documents form a decoration piece on the shelves of the offices. The further activation of these schemes, depend on the aptitudinal interest and intelligence level of your minister. The voice of electorate and the awareness of people can also, put the government machinery to shed callousness and the interrogative three w's, find the mind-set of the minister on the right track, otherwise the welfare schemes would taste the sweet and sour combination to get the knots and twists removed to trace its way to the implementation level.

IFS AND BUTS

The bureaucracy too, is very selective to implement such schemes, but the word "if" and "but" when incorporated by the bureaucrats in memorandums of articles, put the whole plan out of gear. These selfless servants may also extend their valuable suggestion to the Netas, to visit some advanced country, to chisel up their genius, to give impetus to the welfare schemes. The idea obviously would find an immediate concurrence of not only the honourable Minister but also of his family members or even his near relatives. So this political pick-nick would put the work of implementation of welfare schemes on the lag. The norms for exercising your prudance in tapping off the exchequere would be flouted, and the spirit of oath would be dented too. It would also stem into the war of wits, between the audit and ministerial set up. The minister would now be busy in tapping off all the possibilities and probabilities to save his face. His time would be consumed in removing the dust from "Why, where and when" and the bureaucrats would try to magnify all "Ifs & Buts". Now who would be interested in implementation of welfare schemes. Thus the percept remains a percept, and the practice would not even be hallowed by their masters.

This type of selfless service, is now the general cross talk of the public.

Now the general epithet used by the Netas, is that they would go to the people's court at the time of hustings. Some tempting slogans would be devised again, to be shouted at all opportune times and lectures on moralities would be delivered by such shadowed Netas. The man's common sense would stand mocked at and defeated. His instinctive co-ordination would go haywire, and his mental apparatus would pause for resuscition of his depleting beliefs in the system. Even the flower plants, which lost their fragrance in making beads for such Netas, would be left fending for the miscalculations of their Malis.

THE RELIGIOUS, PERCEPTION AND THEIR ACTUALISM

The kow-tows and the dynamics of all the religious preachers mostly converge on one point that the man must recognise his ownself, must see what is "I" in the macrocosm of our existence. In this process they advise the man to have divinely options only, while aspiring for worldly persuits. Renunciation, discrimination, vavek, company of mystics, the man is advised to have. Helping to needy, chastity in spending and live in communion with all pervading inner light. They also lay too much stress on, shedding the effects of Maya. From Maya, they mean the people to remain aloof and not be tempted to the material wealth. The man must exercise control over his sensual desires and remain in the service of humanity, as the God abodes in human beings, rather all beings are its manifestations.

So, said and written are superb, and an open license, to liberty, emancipation and salvation. Now the thought provoking part starts.

These people, who give discourses to the turbulated souls, they themselves mostly accentuate their attributes, which are diagonally opposite to their sermons. They opt their own conduct, as if the Almighty has given them the choice to act according to the dictates of their mind. Their pose, pause and perversity are alright outwardly but their internal travesteries are not better than the ordinary people. Their practices and percepts are not on the same padestal.

There are preachers whose engagement for one hour by an ordinary man on some social function, make the poor man to reavaluate the off repeated adjectives as selfless, lustless etc. by the preachers, focussing on the renunciation of worldly persuits. The monetary compensation desired by him, goes out of reach of the poor man and his chain of thoughts is signalled, a caution, by his intelligence, to read the dotted lined words on some vehicle as, 'Hutt-Puchhe" that is (get lost). There comes a natural stroke over his head, in assertion consciously or unconsciously, which points towards the hypocracy and hollowness of the perceptions and practical mind-sets of these people. His search of finding solace and some peace of mind to his already furnaced conscious, gets a jolt and the grinding mills, of the compulsions of environment put him to more furious turbulations. The unending pressures accentuated by the daily visits and torques of circumstances, make the reflexes of his face more explicit which very often shatter his belief in the voidness of the religious priesthood.

The written scriptures being used by the modern times priesthood, have been written from the insight of accomplished men in our culture, who were the pillers of our heritage and were really ethical and stood testimony to morality, simplicity, renunciation, discrimination, selfless service, truth, compassion, devotion, purity other divinely qualities. Those ecstatic practiced their scriptures to the limits of maximas and even a microscopic fraction of aberaison in any compartment of divinity rendered them infructuous and infarcted in the hierarchy of divine abodes. Their actions and guidance to the worldly people made them Devtas and brought them to riddance and salvation. They were made to follow the drives and derivatives their deeds and the calculi of their projections, and thus they became instruments of a sample social structures of our country. One Sufi Faqir of Islamic sect while describing the pros and cons of man's desires and action in the context of achieving their goals in life, said, to the practitioner:

"Tere Karam Mein Kammi Nahen Karim Hai Tu

Tere Arzoo Ne Hi Tujh Ko Bandda Bana Rakha Hai"

that is (oh man you are an embodiment of Godhead yourself, san, your worldly desires)

They were effective as their practices and percepts were in phase with. Their bodies created an aura of benevolence and brought peace to the peoples minds.

Now when the civilization is gauged as farely advanced, and there is no dearth of religious institutions and organisations, which are busy day and night, extending and imparting lessons on morality, the values are depleting, as the man of an ordinary prudence even, is getting mentally polluted, when he sees that not only the men of pelf and power, but also the modern preachers whom the people consider as the walking morals, are subservient only to worldly desires and the essence of their practical conduct is nothing but mercenary. To collect money and material is their creed. Their high-level gadgets and sky rocketing palatial buildings and their frequent tours and travels to dollars and pound sterling, control and command countries, speak of the spirit of renunciation and chastity, being mouled by these very walking morals of our country.

Their priorities for these lands, where the social set up is adequately pro people, and where such preaching are least desired points towards their love for material wealth only. The suffering of our own people under deluge of miseries are not their imperatives.

Moreover the land of African continent are almost alien and are untouchable to them, even if the humanity there stands aggressively bruised and torchered, devoid of all ethics and civic behaviour. The state powers arc infested with invidious social systems, hunger, poverty, drudgery, and mal-neutritions are well entrenched. On the face of it, no body even cavil and carp for their emancipation. Is it not an encroachment of the spirit of slogan "that all be blessed" ?

SCIENTISTS AND TECHNOCRATS

In the actual schemes of advancements of developing countries, this category has a special roles for the success and failures of new innovations and inventive projects.

The developing nations may lack in providing proper infrastructures for the time bound social schemes, but this community should try to adjust their projects as per the compatibility and resources of their nation, rather than to desanctify their oath of faithfulness and dedication, while patronising the schemes of other countries.

Their talents and aptitudes have been nourished by the colleges and universities of their own country, and the laboratories and work-stations have sprouted new grooves in their mental apparatus. Leaving our own people, to find better working environments and infrastructures, makes this category, a commercial commodity and leaves an impression that this embodied excellence does not possess a soul, which may breath for its own country. They apprise to weigh the sacrifices of their mother in terms of money. However high titles they may hold, their worth is nothing, in the eyes of their own people.

In contrast to this, whatever our own country, may provide them, within the framework of its resources, would boost their spirit to jump into an era of glory and genuineness. The scientists would be privileged to be stamped by the insignias and titles conferred on them by their nation. They would thus be called a proud asset of their country.

To put one's talents on sale may make you earn a millions or billions in alien lands, but your basic plus mindedness would be totally nullified. In addition to setting up a bad precedent, for the budding genius of your country, you will be weighed with an optimism of sustained prejudices at the general gatherings over a cup of coffee. You will feel to have lost something precious in yourself.

Let me now discuss, something about the successes and failures of your new innovations.

A scholar, Dr. Shuller, says that "A success is never certain and a failure is never final". This is an accepted truth in the dynamics of possibilities. If you have a genius you will succeed in your prototype sooner or later. May be, success may embrace you, sooner, in your own environments and may play truancy even in an ideal infrastructure. So it stands to reason that mistrust and moral turpitudes should not be accentuated to have one's inflated ambitions satisfied, at the cost of your national interest.

On the national plane this category of professionals, who are in the active service of the Government, are not held in high esteem by the people, because most of them generally made the headlines of newspapers, due to their shady characters. They work more to the dictates of their senses, rather than the voice of their consciousness. Some people do create such a mess of their activities, that even the people, with some sense of responsibility also become murkious and shadowy. Even they become instrumental in making their family members and children as vagabonds and unworthy of being called good citizens. They watch an easy flow of money in their homes and hence the dignity of labour and hard work becomes a first causality with such families. The wives and children of such people too are seen using an extra constitutional powers, which ultimately reflect on the reputation of such officers. This factor is common in all categories of Government officers and is a very very vital drag in the implementation of pro-people plans.

We are now living in the times, when news of scams, kick backs, money laundering are the daily headlines of the newspapers and the investigating agencies and judiciary, are totally outstripped to negotiate with such unlawful activities, which take so many twist and turns, in the application of legal codes and are also time-consuming. The legal system is so bankrupt, that the culprit or criminal manages to pull the proceedings in a way that it takes decades to meet the ends of justice, where in the prosecuting agencies, are put to so many pulls and pressures that on many occasions the culprit not only goes scot free, but also recovers his salaries, arrears and promotions retrospectively. This sort of trends, open up the escape-roots for all present and future wrong doers and also put the exchequers to squeeze out a good quantum of money from the coffers of the Government.

The many fold increase in the needs of the people, have tempted so many persons to put their oaths of dignity of law, and constitution, to abuse, which has inflated the number of wrong doers, the responses to the public pressure, to curb such tendencies are too scant, even the wings of the law are also pruned by the men in power, the soul of the people bleets, but who cares ?

The core content of the national mind is standing astounded and scared, while the ambit of the stink in the system is widening. Only some herculen effort, may pull the cart out of the rickety roads, to save the cultural heritage of this pious and pure land of Buddha, Ram and Nanak, to bring it in tune with the spirit of supremacy as before, to rhyme it again as,

"Sare Jahan Se Achha Hindustan Hamara".

4

RIGHTS AND RESPONSIBILITIES

This is a subject which makes the reflexes of a nation or a country a little bit clear in the prismatic reflections of the international behaviour. It is judged in the relative variables, in the political chess of the nations and directly effects the endeavours and achievements of their citizens.

The cosmopolitan structure of the megalopolis is the latest step in our long walk towards complex urban settlements. We can see the citizens of most of the countries amongst us, who interact with our people in all spheres of life. Our assessing eyes and instinctive judgments give us, their dress-codes, their colours, their physical features, their pronunciations of language, their food habits, their social behaviour, their 'Use me' culture etc.

Similarly they walk with their eyes open, and watch our activities, at our homes, at our festivals, our mob-culture (Mobocracy), our standard of living, our responsibilities to our country our civic sense, the conduct of our services and bureaucrats our spitting and scattering habits, the quality of our products, our marketing persuation-poses, our traffic sense, our religious and national festivals and above all, the news headlines of our national papers and magazines, and commentary on our present leadership by the electronics-media.

When this planet is ushering in twenty first century now, the above noted features of all the countries are open to judgment of all.

Taking my own country, one may say that urban population is not more than 26% of its total, but it is more than sufficient to give a sample representation to the world, on our chequered behaviour patterns. Our urban cities too are rural based, as the people living in the cities are also having their roots in the rural India.

As per the imperatives and compulsions of the changing profiles of our culture, the creamy layers in rural society are attracted to the cities, because the cities are environmentally more suited to meet the educational, cultural, medical, ecological, architectural, vocational and all type of other carrier-oriented openings. Moreover the industrial revolution, has drawn an unprecedented number of people into cities. It is therefore obvious that activities and interaction with the cosmopolitan characters of our big cities is a bipolar opening to compare and judge the other nations on all their acute and obtuse planes of civil organisational set ups.

All the above complex observations do emanate from the equivalent effects, of the activities of the people, which are formed by a bit-by-bit responses of the individual.

Responsibilities of the state's power, to funnel up better resources for its citizens, partly depends upon the density of population, in a country and partly on the awareness of its people to feel their full involvement, in getting the infrastructures created by their Governments. But the things become problematic when their citizens become self-centred and the interests of the country are left to the states. It is here that chaotic conditions do take prominence. The rights of the citizens are projected through wrong reflections and do take an unimportant dominance, while the paradoxical reflections of responsible citizenship are unnecessarily deviated. Hence the balance between rights and responsibilities is badly shaken. The rights take precedent on responsibilities, hence the system is desynchronised and law of the land stands to bear the frontal attacks.

The city dwellers tend to have higher standards of living

and better health than rural residents, but when cities grow faster their economies and infrastructures feel hard pressed to meet the needs of the people. The population density, the traffic density and emergence of slum areas, put pressure on general amenities, as electricity, water supply, sewerage, roads, environmental and ecological balances etc. for general consensus. I would try to discuss each point separately.

POPULATION DENSITY

As discussed above, the population in urban areas is increasing at the rate of 39% of total population. The national geographical society depicts that in the year 1947, the year of independence, India had a 350 millions people, and fifty years later, i.e. in 1997, it is about to reach one billion, and it is still projected to become the world's most populous country by 2050. It is quite obvious that even the best designed cities are now feeling the pinch of, overcrowding in traffic, encroachment of Government/Municipal Corporation lands, pressure on water supply and electric supply systems.

To meet his daily needs, the paradoxical projections of human mind are tending too much to self interest. May it be a migrant labour or a well up resident of a city, the common factor, they are opting is, "Self-before state". The general attitudinal inclination, is, to directly apply all possible multiples for their rights and inversely apply the same multiples for their responsibilities. This approach is a major irritant for peace and prosperity of a nation as a whole.

MIGRANT LABOURER

His first and foremost endeavour is to construct a temporary hut by illegally occupying the land of Government or corporation. Subsequently he would tap off the power line to extract electricity, and would also interfere with the water supply system. Taking a queue from him, more and more people in this category would follow the suit and within a span of about ten days, there would appear a cluster of huts. With due regard, I would say that a new pattern of standards would be explicitly visible to the people, which would depict the level of intelligence of these people, and also the specimen of such helmets, would represent the way of living of these people.

As these helmets are right in the vicinities of the urban limits, and the occupants do earn their living on doing some odd jobs as daily labourers, the interaction of their mindswork towards acquisition of materials, to satisfy their sensual desires, as they witness in the houses of well-to-do people.

I may be excused for my humble submission that these people, who play a major role in the constructional activities and are instrumental in making the infrastructures look aesthetically attractive to the eyes are mentally not well versed to judge the things in the right perspective, rather they are tempted to short cuts and are an easy prey to material desires. They are therefore vulnerable to undesirable practices. They are seen going out of their ways to get their instincts satisfied.

If some one happens to pass through the slum areas, the first encounter, he will exercise in the stink of dirt, rubbish, dirty water-pools, mosquitoes, flies, excreta, naked children, half naked women, rickety hair, dark and dungeoned huts, some cattle sheds, stray dogs and multi-amplitudinal spoken-dialect. So to say that they people are totally attuned to create and live in such environments. But despite the poor living conditions, the T.V. antennae are found installed almost on every hut. There may be a few having got V.C.R., V.C.P. also.

This may put one to pause and ponder for sometime, to judge that how the mind of a man remains in subjugation to his sensual desires.

One may not agree with me, but the intensity of sensual dictates, for lower levels of intelligence, cascaded by the effects of lust and love, is more or less the same. Everybody is tempted to this syndrome of unison with realism, and of being nearer to the source of life. Possessing a T.V. set even by a slum dweller is a sufficient evidence to prove this dictum. The poor man may not be able to bulge out the curves of the abdomens of his family members, by providing them with two square meals, but to satisfy his instincts and passions, by watching the late night movies, are his first imperative. The core content of such movies, are lustful and sensuous and hence are in tune with the attributes and afflictions of the lower mind. Factually these may be toxic and harmful for grown up, adolescent minds, but to insulate them from this causal pollutant under the one roomed shelter, is their compulsion.

The sum total equivalent of such living may nurture and breed several types of sustained invectives in the minds of the young one's and may make them vulnerable to unsocial and immoral acts, which ultimately affect the smooth flow of social contours and pollute the civic behaviour, produce so many hysterical characters, who very often end up as hardened criminals.

The state-power and Government planners do initiate some schemes, to mitigate the sufferings of the slum-dwellers, with the ideas of eliminating this menace of unauthorised encroachments and their subsequent effects. They provide them with well constructed one room houses with all other allied amenities, but they people dispose them off, for good monetary benefits and again adopt the same modus operandi, on new Government lands, so the cycle goes on.

If the state authorities try to demolish these unauthorised constructions, they people form a mob and raise hue and cry, helped by certain political parties, who want to gain popularity and make such people their committed vote bank. Thus these people adopt such tactics and say that their rights are being trudged by the Government. But their violations on Government land and its amenities as discussed above, are not their responsibility. I would say without hesitation that this type of cybernetics in our democratic form of Governance, sarcastically doubts human sincerity, as the degree of maturity and understanding of each individual voters is not on the equal level.

One more very important irresponsible act of these people, is to let loose their live stocks during night hours, which in addition to become a traffic hazard, also muzzle down the grassy lawns and plants of the people and thus destroy all the aesthetics and artistic interests. The cattle are found sitting right in the centre of the well-carpeted roads, without any alertness what-so-ever. Even the estates department seems to be helpless to control this menace.

The above discussion is generous enough to give brief hints on how the rights and responsibilities work in the minds of this category of people.

GENERAL URBAN POPULACE

As discussed earlier, about 26% of the total Indian population is living in the cities because of better facilities available in all spheres as compared to rural areas. The level of life expectancy also stands at 63 years, due to better environmental conditions, which have contributed to the population density curve as taking a steep rise. So with this population explosion, the country is confronted with so many problem also.

In furtherance of my discussion on rights and responsibilities, I feel that even the educated families, which are considered to be the nerve centre of the urban life, stand on the same level, so far as the vitalities and vexations of society are concerned. The self interest receives a preferential helo, in the backdrop of national viabilities.

The general trend of city people, does not patronise the balanced equilibrium of plans which are stamped as sanctified by the designers and planners, to promote a smooth flow of civic life, rather they feel pleasure in disturbing the synchronous characters of constructed houses, according to their own whims, to the detriment of the general public. The outer boundaries of most of the houses are found surrounded by the expended metal mesh, by violating the roadberms, which is being used by the house owners as a parking points for their vehicles or is being used for kitchen gardens or as an extension their grassy lawns. The exit of about 98% of houses, having their backs on the main road, are now a most obnoxious violation which covers the walking pavements, being used as displaying spot, for some commercial items, as furniture pieces, cement sacks and bricks, repair shops for scooters, motor cycles and have occupied the areas for eateries and tea stalls. Big hoardings pointing precisely the purpose for which a particular corner is being used are the general eye sore to the passing traffic. The abuse of the bye-laws is so intense and addictive that even a few who are respecting the limits of Government limitations are also tempted join this refrain.

In heart of heart, every body confesses that it is a violation of bye-laws and is punishable under law, but still when some upright D.M. takes action against these violations, the people begin agitating and bring in every thing to trade in the charges, against the Government, that they are depriving so many people, of their vocations, who earn their livelihood for their sustenance, in these hard times. Again the opposition parties stand on their side and rest of the episode ends in the same tactical frame.

Even the public parks, and empty plots become source of foul smell, as the urbanites take it as their esteemed right to throw waste and rubbish in their corners, which make the animals and birds, to flock on such points. Stink, foul smell and scattered waste are the environmental assets of the irresponsible projections of people's behaviour. Even the sanitation employees keep on napping and in some cases too callous and complacent to remove such piles of garbage as a routine. May be a casual halo once a week or so, make these sites to bear a new look. It is also generally seen that the women serving as a domestic help in some houses are instrumental in throwing the packs of waste material on the road, and the rest of the generalities are taken care of by pigs, stray dogs and crows, to make it attuned to our temperaments. So all such trends and tendencies are well assimilated in our psyche, which with the help of political opportunism, make the legal action redundant.

RURAL BEHAVIOUR

In the formation of Governments, the ruralities have more say in the democratic form of Governance. As history stands evidence to it, that most of the legislators and ministers who rule the roost, are from rural background. It stands to reason also, because 74% of the population lives in villages. However the percepts and practices are the same, rather the class consciousness is more vibrant in ruralities. The power of Government and the controls and commands of all succulent out lets, right upto the Panchayat level, are pro-dominance. Obviously this system of sustained cyber potentials shower favours on their kiths and kins, by twisting rules and regulation to their interests.

So in rural areas too, all opportunities are grabbed by the law-makers and law-protectors who work as supplement to each other. The common village Panchayat lands, loans subsidies and other economic shoots or benefits, appropriated for 'have nots' are usurped by predominant elements and their co-relates, while the deserving one's are fed on empty succulent slogans, to hold their aberration annihilated, till the circumstances are changed. So the rights of the poor are predicated to power and all types of, cavil and carp, are brushed aside. The passage of time also helps in burying down all the ill-will and invidious under-currents, created by the illusions of their minds. So this tempo of violations and abuse of power, often goes unheeded in the eyes of justice.

In addition to this, an illegal extraction of power from the power lines, tapping of water distributaries and irrigation-channels, usurping of forest and P.W.D. lands, disturbing ecological balances etc. are out of the preamble of their violation list. So there should be no mental slip in one's mind, to see any deviation in the congruent behaviour of rural or urban mind-set.

COMMERCIAL THOUGHT

This factor is equally crested in the minds of the people, of rural or urban origin. A farmer, a milkman, a grocer, an industrialist or even a way-side stall holder, non of them attach any importance to the health of the people, rather they stress their mental imaginations to find ways and means to pocket as much money as they can, by adulterating the original contents. Outwardly they are religiously disciplined, but the inner recesses of their minds are mercenary to the core.

A farmer knows that the medicines sprayed over the vegetables and fruits are venomous and injurious to health, if brought to market before a week after spray, but he never cares for this. Even the vegetables like the cauliflower are immersed in a poisonous liquid after plucking, but before taking to market, because it bears a fine and fresh look after a dip in that medicine. But it is very very harmful for human consumption. The farmer also knows it, as he uses the medicine under instructions of some responsible employee and he would read the instructions on the label also, but he sells it in the market as it fetches him some more money. The spirit of the great scientists like Louis Pasteur and his subsequent followers stand abused, and their beliefs bruised, who through their discoveries brought out the facts that micro-organism in the food articles cause diseases, and brought out some medicines also, to avoid the injurious effects with proper guidelines. But the misuse of his discovery may also suffocate humanity for some pieces of money.

The same mind-set inspired the milk-vendor to mix water in the milk previously, but now some unscrupulous endeavors have paved a way for these people, in which the so-called synthetic milk, is being prepared and sold, by mixing some ingredients as some detergent, some sugar etc. (I do not remember all the things used as active agents). Not long ago, I read, in the newspapers, that this milk was flowing in the drains of some cities of Uttar Pardesh, when the news of Government raids were leaked out about one hour or so, before its actual execution.

In the last six months of year 1998 the news in dropsy deaths, created by the adulteration of some brands of mustard oil, graced the first page headlines. The use of fats of pigs and some other animals, also do find favours with the adulterators of edible oil.

The news of mad-cows, butchered in the boiteries of Britain, which had a severe effect on the health syndromes who used their meat and other by-products, as food, are still fresh in the esteemed awareness of the world memory. The voice of the masses attuned to such sarcastic and sullen protest, that they had to close down their boiteries. The debate on this subject also held the money mongering tendencies of man, by trying to different types of vulpine discretions to get more meat from the cows. Thus the proxy feeding of cows in contravention to natural law, made a caustic change in the biological metabolism of the animal, which made their cerebral contents open to accentricity and mal-functioning of brains.

So this action of even an enlightened and developed nation stands evidence to the avarice of a man who tried to exercise its authority on the natural law, resulting in the madness of the poor creatures.

The money laundering race in our country has attained to such potentials, that each and every entrepreneur in commerce and trade is infested with this bug. Before starting his business, he will first probe as to what are the cushioned choices of adulteration. Hence the commodities like, wheat flour, spices, red chillies, black peppers, pulses, sugar, oils etc are all under a cross-talk of the people, as to what degree, the human dynamics have been able, to pollute these articles.

Very recently, we had gone through an episode of money hunting postures of vegetable traders, who exercised their rights to hoarding and thus let the prices of onions to shoot upto Rs. 60.00/kg. Virtually this item went out of the reach of the common man and even the middle class families had stopped its use in their kitchens. The Government had tried to avert its responsibility, by incorporating the forced majeur clause, because of the incessant rains in the catchment areas of onion producing states, but 80% of the probable causes were man made. Because of this very complacent and unresponsive attitude of the ruling party, the people have shown them the exit in recent polling in three states.

Before concluding, I would express my anguish in the behaviour pattern of officialdom, who enjoy so many privileges and perks, but do not work to discharge their duties honestly and diligently at all. Honesty compels me to say that to get any official formality cleared in almost all Government offices, needs some accelerating aids, otherwise all types of flimsy objections, under the pretext of safeguard to rules, are abbreviated in the start and finish of ifs" and "buts" on the chains of noting sheets. After several twists covering legal and illegal trajectories, if some one may get his case cleared, he thanks his stars. The actual levers of officialdom work more in reverse gears and less to positive achievements. This abuse of faithful discharge of official duties is covered by the law of protection for trade unionism, and hence even the upright bureaucrats are left redundant before the pressures of "Zindabad, Murdabad" by the slogan shouting employees. So the Turvy Curvy syndrome goes on the same pitch.

In the above discussion, I had tried to brief the readers, how almost all cross sections of society, from zenith heights to zeroedlevels are busy in claiming all ill-conceptions as their rights, but to imbibe assertive reflexes for their responsibilities too, is their psychic refrain. This type of unbalanced attitude in the general civic behaviour, generates unnecessary torques and twists which create undesired ripples in our ethical contours. The talk of Ram Rajya by our leaders, seems to be hollow and ineffective, because the general mind-set of the helms men now, is to acquire and collect as much material wealth as they can, during their tenure of controls and commands. The written code of conduct in our shastras and even in our constitution are actually sweating out at their abuse, by the majority of our Netas, who are hound and are under oath of faithfulness and sincerity to our nation.

Such people are now the walking violators of their responsibilities and have set tone which has vitiated the environments to a rat-race to achieve and acquire whatever material gains one can.

5

SIMPLICITY TO SIMULATION

Simplicity is an essence of life, which is based on the three isosceles constants of existential prism of creation by nature. It helps the man to squeeze his sensual desires to the barest minimum, in which the vertex of illusions mothered by avaricial instinctive ripples of human mind (Tamsik leaning), stands mystified by the forces of moralities. This is the result of one's esteemed awareness to consciousness absolute, practiced by one's mind in perfect surrender to intelligence. The sustaining level, of course, is subject to one's capacity; to assimilate the rationals of existence and its continuous practice in all spheres of worldly pursuits. This is the effective equivalent of human percepts, practiced in the company of wisemen. Without which this divine attribute may not find a permanent slot in the mental digestion of the practitioner.

It should be kept in mind, that even an instant aberration of mind may put the whole show to degradation in the world of simplicity, piousness and wisdom. So a person must remain cautious and composed through out his journey of life.

This subtle sublimation of wisdom with cascading effects of knowledge, practiced as a routine by wise men, plays a vital role in molding the characters of other people (who interact with them) who get inspiration to become constructive players in structuring a healthy society. This essentially becomes a basic input, to boost up the spirit of intemperance and casting the concepts of assertive reflexes in the multifaceted predication of daily needs. It promotes a syndrome of chastity, renunciation, and semblance, to maintain homes and hearths, without an awesome or superfluous tones of extravagance. The hawkish eyes of simplicity and wisdom shed tears even if a single kernel of wheat is bruised, when above 35% of people go to sleep without food.

Not long ago, the father of our nation Mahatma Gandhi and one of our ex-prime ministers Sh. Lal Bahadur Shastri, were the walking apostles of simplicity, serenity, chastity and renunciation. They produced their own wheat, in their small plots, to fill up their body-needs. Also they prepared their own khadi cloth to cover their bodies. Thus they sustained a sentimental legacy of our traditions in holding the dignity of labour in the high esteems. They were patriots and par-excellence were, an embodiment of devotion service, compassion, purity, simplicity honesty, etc. In their lives, our nation remained under the influences of their aura, hence our core characters too were inclined to simple living.

Now the times have changed and our people in general have been stung by the bug of selfishness and commercial thought. The satellite transmissions on the small screen watched daily by the people in their houses, has created such a mix of hotch-potch cultures, that the people are cosying up under the deluge of ultra-modernity, superfluous show of money and mod-cat culture, which are the choicest food for the cult of simulation and hypocracy. Even the people having deep convictions for our heritage had sustained cumulative dents in their practical activism.

As a matter of fact, a simple living is always conjugated with high thinking. So the necessary imperatives of simplicity are, that one should imbibe simplicity in all compartments of one's life. Simple eating, simple clothes, purity of thought and action purity in utterance, purity in hearing, chaste spending, renunciation of material wealth and so on. Actually the pure thought supported by pure activism cannot be bound in adjectival orbits of probabilities.

It is obvious, that the mind of a man, if allowed an

unbridled freedom, will take him to sensual desires, which are unlimited and cannot be satisfied. One can satisfy a hungry-man, but the greed is invincible.

Simulation is a subject of immaturity and lack of knowledge. The wisdom level of general populace not being so high, the communicative modules of their brains would guide them to delusion and delirium. When the civilization has reached, such a cross, where from, all roads lead to extravagance and false kowtow culture, the person having an ordinary prudence naturally falls a victim to simulate cult.

Upto early sixties when electronics media was not a house hold succulent need, the people lived within the ambit of their original culture. They were free from apparent effects of alien customs and their way of living in all compartments of their lives. There developments went in the reflexes of their original environments, but with the advent of T.V. and other electronics gadgets, alongwith several numbers of communication channels, through satellites the life pattern and all types of technological developments have become transparent. The minds of the general public is not selective to choose the educational and knowledgeable programmes, rather they mostly remain glued to the small screen, watching only entertaining programmes, alongwith the dress codes, glamour, dining codes, club and pub culture, hi-bye-chatters, geometrics of pop culture-dance etc. All these programmes are punctuated with commercial advertisements of dress materials, ready made garments, fast foods, cook wares, variety of shoe wears, vehicles, watches, electronics gadgets, house hold appliances alongwith spicy slogan, well designed and documented-performance-projections, presented by glamorous men and women in the back drop. Work as a catalytic agent to put the viewers brain to hysterical hypocracy. The cybernetics of the communicative modules of a person make his thinking redundant to intemperance, and activate the illusions of his mind, which ultimately mar the sedate. Serene and Solemn contents of intellect and take the person nearer to simulation.

I have tried to bring home my point under discussion, in the context, of the effects and imprints left by the small screen in promoting this culture. But the seriousness of its applicability depend upon the individual aptitude. There is not the least shadow of doubt that the satellite communications being monitored on the T.V. screens in our houses, have played a major role in bridging the gap of knowledge, on so many discoveries and inventions, and the people are now, more aware about the graphics of world problems due to the population explosions. The planner and ideologues are now busy to check list the prospective spectrum of twenty first century. They are probing to incorporate their managerial skills on international forums, to confront the probable catastrophic developments.

It is estimated that in spite of the measures taken by the different countries on family planning, the population of the planet is still increasing by more than 80 millions a year. The television screen is helping in giving such statistics to the people by displaying the satellite pictures on population density and the infrastructures to meet with the needs of the people in prospect. Moreover the channels like discovery and commentaries on ecological balances, and the secrets of the down-earth changes and many other knowledgeable aids to thinkers and planners, are an asset to the mankind by this momentous feat of science and technology. But majority of the viewers who remain on the fore-front of the sociological centre stage do not show much interest in such programmes.

The majority of the adolescent viewers and their elder even, are attracted to the same very commercial glut and the juicy display of hi-fi culture only, which naturally works on diametrically opposite themes to simplicity and serenity.

PROMOTING AIDS OF SIMULATION

Until and unless, an individual mind has got sustained convictions, deeply embedded in the cosmic recesses of his common sense, the floating and fluxuous tendencies would lead him to the logistics of relative cushions, which would tempt him, to down cast the up manship, of his relatives or neighbours. The race of up manship is very acutely felt in certain families, which is zoomed to acquire certain gadgets after seeing the commercial advertisements on the small screen. This tendency to feel concerned in sociological culverts is more pronounced in ladies, who lack in knowing the grace of simplicity and judicial use of hard earned money. Their poor understanding of pathetic condition of human beings, who are not fortunate enough even to have one glass of clean drinking water in a day, is simply sinful and unpardonable. Such show of wealth is to play joke with the millions of toiling masses, on this planet. If some one is fortunate to have possessed some means, he should he wise enough to control his needless desires, in order to put a stop, on his averical temperament. This is a major malady in the possibilities of relative sociological behaviour. It should be curbed by exercising an intense temperance to stop this rat race.

The commercial advts. given in the T.V. programmes, boost the tangential pricks and provoke the unmatured minds to loosen the strings of their purses, which inflate the coffers of the trading houses. Even an article, not of much importance is presented in such gimmickry twists and persuasive aids, that the so called new found relic, is found majestically decorated on your self, on first opportune outing to the market. Even a package of dingy-grass, named as broom for cleaning the floor of your house, shown in the hands of some mercurial and glamorous lady, with attractive and operative sequential poses, tempts the house-ladies try their hand on it. To give maximum coverage to such commercial advertisements based on their documentation and interposing them in some ecstatic serials, depend upon the capacity of the trading house to pay. But how this syndrome is poised to bring this show of false prestige in our people is any body's guess.

ADVICE-VERSES-VICE

It is my humble submission, what I am now advising to the younger generation, the rationals of all these reflexes, I have undergone in my adolescence and in my young age. We, of course, were not so privileged and resourceful to enjoy such environments, as our childhood and adolescence were passed in one roomed mud-house, when even the two square meals were obtained after a very very hard labour and the question of this hi-fi-T.V. culture was never dreamt of by we people. However, so far as the cult of simulation, that is, to show off to others, which you are really not, also prevailed in us. Although the orientation and contents were different as per the specifics of the times, but after all, the cult is cult. Our temperaments too, were wedded to it. We people also wanted to show off rather to let the people judge, as to where we stand. There is a beauty in being known, rather than to say, "please know us".

The level of our dealings to achieve our self interests too, were according to the compulsions of the time, but the temperamental pricks and persuasions were the same. The life long experience of a man, provides him a gist of merits and demerits which the old generation shares, with their off springs, I also admit that such advices are extended at a stage, when their own sensual desires and faculties instincts, start assuming reversal hysterises. A Punjabi young man, after reading these lines can concur it with a Punjabi satire as under:

(Jaddon Mukk Gai, Gharay De Dane Te Bun Gai Singh Sabhiey)

"that is when all the faculties of a man are weakened and are rendered in operative he then turns to religion and servitude".

A very correct and factual situation in all its actualism and accentuations. But even the above noted epithet, through which all persons pass, cannot make any dent in the simplistic orientations, as it never looses its sanctity, what-so-ever be the vicissitudes and set ups.

My memory is also divulging a few lines from some one, which emerge from the deep recesses of one's consciousness. That all the hustle and bustle hello and hi of modern era, supported by all types of comforts and cosy consolations in the city are nil before, simple, sedate and up-rightness of the village life. The Urdu couplet in support of this is some thing like this:

Gaon Pahunche Shehar Se, To Sadgi Achhi Lagi,

Ghar Mein Jalte, Diyay Ke Roshani Achhi Lagi,

Bassi Roti Sek Kar, Jo Maa Ne, Nashte Mein Di

To Har Ameeri Se, Mujhe, Yeh Mufalsi Achhi Lagi

I think the content of this couplet is correct but who composed it, I do not know. Any way its incorporation in my mind is, that "when I reached my village from the city the straight forwardness of villager gave a soothing effect to my mind. So much so, even the light of the earthen lamp brought me nearer to reality. In the morning, a simple venture of my mother conferred upon me a deluge of affection, when she served me with a stale bread after heating it on the baking plate, on the face of which all the comforts of richness stood paled and down crested. So I think it is an unforgettable tribute to the simple living.

EXPENSIVE PRESENT AND PENSIVE FUTURE

The word "Now" is the minuetetest sublimation of the time dimension. Any moment one reserves to think about "now", the moment loses its slot in the present, and passes on to the past. So the past become incumbent on future. There is no scope of correcting your "now negativism" in the "now' itself. So the pensivity and penance of your negativism, becomes the subject of future.

The life is too dear to be lost in delusion, due to mental derangements and false beliefs. One must learn to put a stop to one's negative thinking, otherwise his future would be under stress and tension, give him a pensive and passive thoughtfulness. In the geometrics of life, one has to weigh the complements and supplements of his needs and necessities on the pragmatic scale that evaluates your assertions solely by the practical consequences.

The priorities of expenditures must be fixed diligently and in sequential descendence, so that our house may not loose its pious epithet of being called a house. I have seen that some houses are so stuffy that they bear a look of a departmental store. Even the pelmets meant for curtains, have been used for placing certain articles as dummy animals mascots, old and worn out antiques etc. The aesthetic look of such houses, is so shabby that the first impression obtained by a new comer is that the expenses of the house are not under the control of experienced hands.

I may be excused, for expressing my views without any reservation, that certain houses are under the control of such an autocratic and imitative natured persons that they are in the habit of spending more than their actual capacity. If they are salaried people, they exhaust their coffers in the very first week of the month and for the rest of month, anxiously await the first day of the next month. Due to their spending habits, they bear a brooding and downcast faces for most of the days, which are the results of their overtures to show off their superiority. Such persons naturally adopt some unfair means to satisfy their whims.

This uncontrolled and unresponsive competitiveness breeds so many other ills and invectitudes, which ultimately make them and other members of family pensive and quarrelsome. The house becomes a ready-made hell and the consequential effects are tension and disputes which may end up in more tragic developments even. It therefore is very necessary that unnecessary spending should be put to an intensive scrutiny with due diligence and spot priorities. The basic criteria should be, that your house look neat and tidy, not a breeding place for moths and cockroaches. Moreover one should follow a thumb rule that his spending does not sensitise the feelings of others, which may give vent to an individuals belief that the sweat of the toiling masses has been laughed at. This can be expected only from a person who possesses the wisdom level, to judge the dignity of hard labour.

So save yourself from mental pollution and pensiveness of your future by planning your present spending to be judicious and justified.

POOH-BAH-CULTURE

I, now want to discuss the adverse effects of unnecessary spending on your off-springs.

The look of a super abundance, of your house creates a very bad impression on the developments of your children. The children feel that the flow of money to their house, is very easy and their tender feelings get attuned to this "Pooh-bah-culture". They assume themselves to have been destined to cyberheight controls in the otherwise, topsy-tury spectrum of modern living. The adolescence and unmatured thinking does not allow them to come out of lolly-pop culture, and they become non-too-good citizens, to face the vagaries and cutthroat competitions of the future life.

The time never stays, and similarly torques and twists of talent, power and authority also do change hands. It never remains the fiefdom of a single family. The history is full of examples, where in the fortunes of people had an 180° turn, during a brief period. It is therefore my simple request that one should always remember that hallucinations of the present time may become a holocaust in the near future.

One more very important under current mostly observed in the street talks of Punjab, regarding the Pooh-bah-cultured families, is stamped with an epithet

(Bhukey Di Dhi Raiji, Te Khey Udaon Laggi)

that is "Only a person of mean character, indulges in superfluous show of power and wealth".

Moreover it is your percept, your knowledge, your simplicity, your purity of thought, your truthfulness, which make you great and you can see straight into the eyes of others. It is therefore advisable that one should not subjugate himself to sensual upheavals in his life, much less fall a prey to the hi-fi and advertisement-additive-syndromes displayed by the electronics media.

If a calf goes and tries to suck the milk of a cow, other than his own mother, it would achieve nothing except some body-blows, from her hind hoofs. Only his own mother-cow, would show affection and love, by oozing out the yearning waves of her milk reservoirs. So without any illusion, one should follow, that our own culture would give us all protection, self confidence and trustworthiness. We must be able to discriminate between our own and alien.

One should see the writings on the walls with open eyes, and try to set one's house in order. It is a sin if one closes his eyes, when he knows that an intense darkness is awaiting him.

One more point is emerging out of my memory is, that our late ex-premier Sh. Lal Bahadur Shastri, did not allow the Air conditioners to be installed in his house, lest his children may not get such environments and in that case, they may find their adjustments, in their future living difficult. He being, even, the top executive did not forget his roots. Was he not aware of this way ward cultures? No it was his level of thinking and his sense of oneness with our people, that he displayed his homely routine as an ordinary Indian. He knew the dignity of labour and hard work. So my stress is only on a point that one should not try to flow with the tide of imposing currents, rather one must stick to his own way of simple and smooth flow in life. So be aware that "Yourself control, will give you unlimited control".

CLUB AND PUB CULTURE

Uptill now I have discussed the adverse effects of T.V. on children and some unmatured elders. There is one more accentric and estrayed escape rout to an alien culture, through clubs and pubs, which is the legacy of the British Empire, and is being exercised by the Indian people, who are under an illusion of their placement in upper strata society.

Their graduation for this culture, is their capacity to lavish spending, on drinking and dancing, to get themselves placed in an apparently most respected category in societical planes.

Such clubs are existing in big cities, where in, the high officials and enterprising entrepreneurs do, gather, in the evening and indulge in all of types fun and frolic, upto the late night hours. The membership fees of these clubs are too high and are out of the reach of the common man. The high officials, who "toss and dot" their noting sheets and take decisions on all types of "ifs" and 'buts", by exercising their powers, which have been delegated to them, as watch-dogs, to protect the spirit of the constitution and law, qualify to become its members, by dint of their identity in the officialdom. Of course it entirely depends on the will and interest, of the officer concerned as to whether he or she wants to join it or not. Most of the officers who do refrain and avoid too much frankness, lest their status may be blemished in officialdom, don't join such clubs. They may be right too as too much intimacy undermines authority, and too, much nearness affects jurisprudence.

Similarly big Industrialists are attracted to its membership, partly to refresh and relax from their grilled routine, and partly to get themselves a bit nearer to the officialdom for their own benefits in the commercial tangram of their business patterns.

The membership of such clubs is open to the couples, and normally both husband and wife, if both are interested, may join it. They leave their wards with the domestic servants or if could be, with some senior members of the family. In Indian clubs, the couples dine and dance, and play certain indoor games. A feeling of cyberheights and an exalts of greatest sorts, is a certainty with the members of such clubs.

The idle gossips, playing of cards, some indoor games, and drinking are the main attributes of the males, while the females keep themselves busy in domestic chatters, and playing of Tambola etc. This is also the choicest place for the ladies to instinctively, judge the dress material and mind-sets, of each other, to the liking and leaning of the well placed bureaucrat's wife, so as to get their own antiquarians replaced with their newfound choices, and to attain the level of their highest co-relate. All these manoeuvres take them nearer to the ultra-modernism and fill up the core content of their mental conceptions with parasitic ingredients which encroach upon the pious and pure recesses of their consciousness. This bi-polar, thinking may destroy their synchronism in simple and pure living and brings home all the prospective demonic diatribes in their family life. The people of club culture generally do not look to their roots and promote simulating tones in all their routines, the consequential results may make them and their children a breed of servile dependents in the competitive world which is now taking a plunge into the 21st century.

Moreover to negotiate with this extra spending, the man sometimes adopts certain foul or fair means, which naturally pollutes his mind. He leaves the normal rhythem of his work-culture and goes astray in defiance to the voice of his consciousness. Such persons cannot be true and sincere toward their duties. They also become instruments to irritate the cerebral modules of so many others, who are affected by such self-styled adoptions of these people.

One more very very shameful fancy of such clubs, which I have read a few months back, in some newspaper, was regarding the swapping of their wives. I am not certain whether it was related to some Indian club or to some club of foreign country, but this news was published in an Indian newspaper. Obviously it must have come to the notice of so many people, and its succulent contents must have found space in their mental digestion also. This type of whimsical overtones are not welcomed in Indian society, which has its inherent origin in the dignified and self-controlled womanhood of Mata Sita, Savitri, Tarawati, Rajni etc. But the sensual desires of uncontrolled minds fall a prey even to this low level of derogation. This is the height of bankruptcy of one's responsibilities and regards, towards the protection of honour of Indian womanhood, to which the man is bound by a pledge of faithfullness and protection of their wives, whatsoever, be the circumstances.

Honesty compels me to say, such an activism which can never suit to our culture, should be discarded with contempt it deserves, otherwise the future genetic sprouts of such yanky-lanky, off break syndromes, would give your society only profligate mimics, who will prove hazardous not only to their parents, but also the nation would feel the hi-cups of their trust-worthiness. They would only assert an unusual style of social conventions, which would impede their careers to meet the challenges of the times ahead.

I conclude my discussion with the humble submission that the lower mind of a person if allowed to go unbridled and unchecked, would always subjugate to the sensual desires and take him to a deluge of hysterical desperation. In that situation even a cushioned-pace-breathing, would not salvage you. Time will look at your past and helplessness may lead you to utter pessimism.

The imperatives of healthy existence demand to be aware and cautious about false beliefs and negativism in your life. As somebody has said "If you do wrong and try to prove, you are right, time will smile at your foolishness".

6

CLEANLINESS TO COCKROACHES

It appears that the explosion in world population, is far ahead of the negotiating limits, of the general infrastructures, meant for the needs of todays civilized world. May be, the developed countries are managing their affairs, with the matching prerequisites, but the under developed countries are definitely under too much strain on this front. Unfortunately the population growth in poor countries are opting an explosive proportions, as compared to the overall global figures. It is obvious therefore that their infrastructures are already out stripped to meet the needs of their people.

As per the population growth of our country its figures stand at 975.3 millions approximately in Oct. 1998. The family planning programmes adopted by the Government in the last three decades have put the people on alert, and the growth has been plummeted dramatically, but still a lot has to be done on this front. The most serious drawback in the implementation of family programme is that, the cross-section of the population, who actually need them, is not properly identified by the Government agencies, rather its implementation is being done under the complex and conspicuous amorous adventures covered under a camouflage. Most of these agencies remained confined to the families who are already aware of it, and the people living in astrayed helmets, in slums and in inaccessible areas, never get any jolt to get themselves out of the deep slumber. There is no justification with our agencies not to achieve the level of fertility rate at level with that of China, i.e. 1.8 per woman as compared to our own at 3.4. China being more populous country than that of ours is far ahead of us, although the level of environmental opportunities are more or less the same.

There is no cut off point to judge as to what extent our country can accommodate this growth, but taking to the tone and temperaments of our people, our atmospheric and agricultural exploits, our sources of irrigation, our Industrial growth, we can apparently say, that in our near future we may strain our cybernetics to intolerable limits. The most important ingredients for sustaining our lives which would bear the brunt on this front, would be fresh air, unpolluted water, clean and ventilated houses and nutritious and unadulterated food articles.

The pivotal point, on which the most of the above inputs, would be monitored and utilized by the people are their villages, cities and scattered helmets. Although the vital energy sources as fresh air, water, sunlight etc. are showered by the nature on all beings, free of cost and without any distinction, but their further checks and controls, by the man made, blows and flows, to satisfy their requirements, have ripped the normal flows of these life-support-system, which have ensured the distortions and denting of these natural blessings. The first causality of such manifestations, is the neatness of the environments and cleanliness of the natures provisions.

How the people in our country look to these problems and how these are affecting their ecological-balances, need a critical observation, which I would try to discuss now.

The basic input of human life is fresh air. No life on earth can exist without oxygen. Food, water, and sunlight, are also very essential, but the breathing exercise in the human and animal life is going on every time. It ceases only when the individual is pronounced as dead. In furtherance of my discussion, I will take up these basic inputs with respect to human beings only.

As discussed in earlier chapters, India is a country, where

most of the people live in villages, where in, the lives of the people are based on different modes of practical and manual works. The dwellings there, are not to any proper plans or designs, rather the houses are constructed on zig zag streets, without even the rudimentary considerations for sunlight, ventilation, drainage, exit and entrance to the houses. To consider about any architectural or aesthetic look, is by far the most, casual option, in the construction manual of village artisans, who help the inhabitants to construct these living cells. Mostly the experience of the individuals, oriented to the existing practices are the basic input in such layouts.

Mostly such dwellings are constructed in a cluster, with sides and back walls adjoining to each other. Hence no windows and ventilators could be possible. The rooms constructed give a look of a behive without any opening, other than the doors meant for the exit and entrance on the front only. No consideration of wind-direction or rays of sunlight, make them as dark and dungeon helmets.

The water sources in the villages were generally some uncovered wells, but now with change of times, the people have installed hand-pumps in their houses. Whether the water is fit for human consumption or not, is not the subject of their minds at all. One more man made malformation in villages, these days is that they had constructed lavatories in their houses, where in, the excretion is absorbed in the deep pits dug out by them. The absorption of all the toxic materials in the porous textures of the earth, does pollute the reservoirs, of water underneath, which are the sources of supply to the water pumps installed for drinking water. The villagers normally have a latent sensibilities to this syndrome and are least bothered about the adverse effects of such manoeuvrabilities. How does this turbulate their health patterns remain out of their comprehension and mental vision, this practice adopted by the people, is summarily affecting their healths, as they are drawing their drinking water, the sources of which fall in the vicinity of such polluted reservoirs. This is an ill-advised facility, randomly adopted by the people without weighing their merits and demerits.

I feel that the source of water, should be more than 100 feet away from the dug out pits, not connected to any systematic-septic-trans-disposal-channels. This can be possible only, where the houses may be spacious and not adjoined to each other, which is a rare possibility in the thickly populated villages.

Regarding the allied problems which emerge from this type of layouts of villages, are the drainage, lanes, mosquitoes, insects etc. The most piquant and stringing conditions, which are a constant eye-sore in the village scenes, is, that no rules or regulations regarding the coverage of lanes are observed. Some lanes are so tight cornered that it is difficult for the users of such lanes to walk through them with their all-important complex carriages of chaffs and other cattle feeds, which cannot be carried to their specific spots, without the topsy-turvy scatterings, which is not only an economic loss, but also becomes a cause of stink and smell after some days. Also it becomes a hatchery for mosquitoes and insects to reproduce their species, similarly there being no proper arrangements for drainage, the waste and dirty water of the houses, are found scattered in the lanes, which spread all its adverse effects, in a waywards, drifts and crifts, in the form of dirty pools, the effects of these unresponsive invectives project the reflections of their jinked laughters, on the defined environments created by the inhabitants themselves.

The situation in small towns and old cities is non-too-good. The people possess small houses in narrow lanes. Some buildings are dangerously poised on their skyward construction, where the population density is too high. The pressure on facilitative infrastructures has already crossed the functional limits and is tightened to the last thread of their control buckles. There are houses in the old cities, the residential rooms, of which have not seen the light of the sun, since decades. Pale and ashen complexes of people stand testimony of their depravity from the sun-light and pollution free breathing air. Such dark and dilapidated houses naturally put more pressures on the Public amenities, as water supplies, electricity and disposal of wastes etc. and also such areas are prone to diseases and other diatribes relating to dense population.

The disposal systems of such towns too, consists of uncovered drains which despite stink and foul smell breeds all types of insects, mosquitoes, cockroaches and reptile living beings. It is quite obvious that such environments are prone to malfunctioning of nature's inputs, which are considered as the health promoting aids. So the cleanliness is again the first causality in the practical contours of the society.

Moreover the constructions and designs of houses in such localities is such that the provisions for the general household, i.e. eatables etc., are open to rapid-action staleness and decomposition. Moreover such houses in the old cities do have their vocational centres in the houses itself, which too contribute to the nook and corner, suffocations with the waste materials from their finishing processes.

The old cities, may be big or small, more or less follow the same living pattern. May there be some variations due to their cultural influences, but the synthesis of probabilities and possibilities in the geographical graphics are at the same level.

Regarding the planned urban developments, the inhabitants enjoy the fancied laid out infrastructures by the government, which is well illustrated in the land scapes of the cities abyss and summits. Such cities are also punctuated with well carpeted roads, parks, markets, controlled traffic, hospitals, entertainment centres, Government offices, modes of transport, Industrial complexes, flyovers, hotels, tourist centres, and all types of cybernetics for infrastructures etc. The houses too are well designed and equipped with all types of facilities.

The layouts and living habits of ruralites and urbanites of big and small cities, have been discussed briefly, but the common factor amongst all is the creation of breeding grounds for cockroaches and insects which is needed to be discussed now.

COCKROACH—CULTURE

As already probed, the electronics media have narrowed the gap of people's living habits. The glut of advertisements being displayed on T.V. are watched and witnessed by all and sundries, big or small, poor or rich. The sensational ripples in these programmes imbibe an optional-tinker in the mind of the people, which affects the marketing probabilities of almost each house and stems in the stuffing off; the kitchen-shelves and stores to an extent that the food items as biscuits, chocolates, toffees, candies etc., keep on lying in the kitchen cabinets for a long time. These items are the fancied temptations of the children who scatter and spoil more and eat less, thereby making the remains of these items entice cockroaches and insects. You will experience that there are safe dens in all nooks and corners, for these impatiently running cockroaches. The damp and dark opening are their choicest breeding spots. This twig-headed voracious dark brown insect, which would make you grim-faced at first sight, is the direct-outcome of profligate habits of the house ladies, which are due to the sustained effects of the publicity on T.V. screens. An oblivious attitude towards the physical work is also responsible to this state of affairs.

One more factor responsible for this pro-cockroach environments, are leftovers of eatables, by the children and negligence of the persons responsible for post-feed care. The children these days too, are all for adoption of a behaviour pattern, as they see in the T.V. advts. It is obvious that their demands are random and they presume as if every thing is available in their kitchen. Houses are being treated as Hotels by these tiny-tots. It is therefore the compulsions of house-hold-managers, to keep every thing in their kitchen shelves and in their stores. But they are found wanting and lacking in picking up the left-overs in the plates or scattered pieces on the ground, which are the fancied choice of cockroaches and insects. In such houses, if you are obliged to switch on, your lights during night hours, you will be thrilled to note down the numbers of these dark-brown-insects, running helter skelter, to hide themselves in the dark and damp openings. Mostly such despicable and despondent quirks, bear a relation with well placed and financially sound houses, where in the ladies shirk doing any domestic jobs with their own hands. It has been seen that in the well placed houses, there are Ayas or domestic servants, who do all cleaning and scrubbing duties. If they fail to turn up some day, which are their common refrain, the cookwares and utensils are kept in wash basins which give a very dirty look, and it provides a cultivation base to cockroaches and insects to grow their species, through experimental growth of micro-organisms. Hence the tidiness of environments in the poor families, who scrub their utensils with dry ash and with their own hands, are markedly well as compared to well-placed society.

Moreover there is a great difference between the finish and finality, if a job got done by your own hands, and, of a work got done by your domestic aids. The general refrain of the employed mind is to do all jobs with performing tricks, that is to perform them to look attractive outwardly. The direct-looking space would have a nice look, but all other nooks and corners would get an incremental push of dirt, by a mere stroke of broom or a floor-scrubbing-flaps. Whatever elocutionary or terse speaking you may do, it would slip over the elliptical cones of their minds and their "As you were" tenors would remain the same. Rather your own eloquence would stand flopped.

There are now so many disinfecting aids available in the market which help in driving away these insects, but these creatures are so acclimatised, that it is difficult to kill or destroy them. Even when we presume that it has died and brush it away, we see that it has again arisen and is running with the same speed. I have seen, the house ladies running after this insect with a shoe in their hand, but its clever twists and twirls play hide and seek, to again enter in some of the openings of your house to continue its polluting and destroying discretions as usual. Even this blady twig-oscillating torturous being, finds its entrance in your boxes and suit cases, to continue its business in cutting, through holes in the layers of your costly garments.

As these unscrupulous burglars, enter your house from their base-camps and protectorates, safely denned in the sewerage and disposal pipes, naturally they carry with them, millions and billions of bacterias and several other organisms, which ultimately spread many diseases and pollute the environments both clinically and ecologically, although their latent effects do not come to the mental vision of the people.

The things now stand at such a cross that no amount of cavil and carp, can retrieve the situation. Neither this automotived culture can accept the Indianised wisdom attributes, which may penetrate into the inner recesses of the people's consciousness, nor the dynamics and diatribes of ultra modernism can be punctuated by any speed-breaking aids.

The economically sound families are now taking up, to use vacuum cleaners and some chemical agents to counter the spread of this menace of cockroaches, but I fear that such remedial measures cannot be taken as a homogeneous adaptation by all the people. The health and sanitary department can have and are using certain fumigations and anti-bacterial aids to eliminate the worst effects of these organisms but even this step will prove only a damp-squib. The purity of environments would now stand victimised, till some prophetic or catastrophic changes may compel people to probe their origins once again.

7

ABUSE OF GURUKUL CONTROLS

Assimilations of the effects of one's experiences in the trials of various means for existential combats, has remained a fervent attraction, since the times of the advent of human development. The degree of the achieved level of prudence, and the capacity to reutilize that level, in practical orientations, to the maximum advantage of one's existence brought the conventional epithet of leadership or head manship of a tribe or a sect. The idea of this head manship may be originated to stone-age, when the human mind was still in primitive abysmal ignorance. With the advancement of civilization, the man entered a stage where in the standard of living needed, the cumulative and collective pit falls of success and failure to be summarily, preserved and transmitted to their future generations. These were the projections of the mediaeval ages when the tribal-lingua-franca, took the driving seat and the cerebral ripples in the mental apparatus of some individuals, became subtle and sublime, who by dint of their experienced adventures and endeavors, used the formations of the local language or demonstrating aids to get their experiences recorded in book forms to be transmitted to the younger generations. Such people were recognised as leaders or Gurus. These were the times when this Guru-Chela, sanctimonism came into existence.

Gurudom at that time was a revered and respected

institution. The Guru was considered as an embodiment of consecration, holiness, free of any sin, a walking moral, free from any sort of transgression of consciousness and a strict observer of divine laws. He was also free from pride, covetousness, lust, anger, envy or sloth etc. A simple life with the barest minimum material needs, was his common refrain.

The kings and the high officials in the kingdoms, sent their wards to the learning centres maintained by the Gurus, which were called Gurukuls. The Gurudom also served as the advisory bodies to the kings, and helped them in managing the affairs of their kingdoms, with utmost care and caution, while considering themselves as the protector and servants of their people. The kings were advised to be divine in their control and commands and lead a simple and renunciated lives. Our history is full of examples, of kings who ruled their people with calm, composed and compassioned minds and even roamed in their kingdoms in disguise, to get the correct backfeeding of how the people felt about their Governance. They did not feel arrogated in case some person in their kingdom spoke ill about any deceptive or deficient adoptions being exercised by their king. Rather they took concrete measures to eliminate all sorts of misgivings and hi-cups being felt by their subjects. The Gurudom was revered and respected so much, that even the great kings, renunciated their every thing, under the guidance of the Gurus and went to the jungles to lead their remaining lives strictly according to the divine laws.

The students who entered these schools were called 'Chelas' in Sanskrit language, and also the medium of instructions were Sanskrit. All the philosophic, political, social sciences and literary books, and marshal arts scripture were in Sanskrit, which were covered in Vedas, Purnas, Samritis and Upanshids to name a few. The main thrust in those days was to accomplish the younger generation in religious and moral ethics. Even the off-springs of some tribes who could not send their wards to Gurukuls were got influenced by the aura of moral waves which encompassed the environments as a whole.

The purity of mind and a sustained and sordid graphics on behaviour patterns, made the students living, specimens of ideal characters. There were no tolerance or resilience cushions allowed. Every student was a moralist to the core. This was because the teachers themselves were accomplished men in all inclinations of existential planes. Even a fraction of negligence in positiveness could render the students to go down the vertex of studentship and enter the band of brats and contemptuous creatures.

The teachers (Gurus) were perfect beings, in their knowledge of yoga, that is, their communions with the consciousness absolute, which lead them to bliss. They lived in clean and healthy environments away from the hustle and bustle of the habitats. Their main abodes were a simple cottage, which was kept absolutely neat and clean. They made their bedding on the floor, covered with the skin of lions, as this bedding was always safe, because all types of reptile life and all other animals, had a natural repulsion to the skin of the lion, and there could be no disturbance, when the practitioners go in communion with their esteem. Their food was too scant as they ate to live only. It consisted of some stray fruits and green leaves of certain herbs. The most of the time, of such mystics was passed, in acastacism. It is recorded in our religious scriptures, that such pure and pious souls, when in acastatic state, went in unison with the infinite, and were showered with a drip of nectar which gave them the necessary vigour and strength. Their faces bore a glowing look and even a common man could not see straight into their eyes, as their eyes emitted an intense light waves.

Such teachers were habitual to rise, at the advent of dawn, called "Brahma Mahurat" and after taking bath they would sit in erect postures and would concentrate on their self-esteem. This way they conquered their minds and recognised their own "I" i.e. "who am I". Nobody could disturbs them during that period as their 'Astral' body would go in sublimation, leaving their material body frame. This was their routine practice to, get to the knowledge of "Self".

They ate very little, wore simple dark yellow robes and had a pair of wooden foot-supports (Pauvas) with a fixture of wooden knob to be supported within the thumb and flengis of their feet. This was the general constitution of their body needs.

Regarding the disciplines followed by the students in the Gurukul. They regarded their teachers as divine descendants and held them in their high esteems. When summoned by the teacher, the student would bow to his teacher with the straight frame of their body, postured as lying parallel to the ground with their hands stretched forward and their head touching the ground. The student will not rise until asked by the Teacher (Guru). This posture is called "Dandwatt Parnam" in Hindi.

After getting blessings of the Guru and after getting order to rise, the student will stand before his teacher with folded hands and would cautiously receive instructions from him. The students were trained to shed all types of self-assertions and egoism, while displaying all humility and humbleness. They were given training from their tender age, to be well-behaved, own simplicity and serenity, discard egoistic tendencies, adopt good qualities in their conduct, make religious percepts as their routine practices, to be true and sincere in all walks of life. Hypocracy, slumber and sloth were the traits contemptuously kept out of their mental-conduits. Dignity of labour, helping the poor and needy, practicing compassion, pin pointed concentration on the job being undertaken, discarding tendencies of upmanship and promoting comradian-supplementations, to be kind to all beings, but being tough, to counter criminality and injustice, imbibing a spirit of self-sacrifice without fear and so many other attributes which could be enshrined in their conduct to make them accomplished human beings were the curriculum of their education.

Their day began at early dawn and after morning chores, they would perform yoga followed by certain hectic acrobatic exercises or games. They would say their prayers and then their teaching would commence.

As discussed above, the main thurst of their education was to mold their pupil's lives, according to the principals enshrined in the religious scriptures, the contents of which contained all types of knowledge based on the subjective projections of the esteemed experiences of our seers. The parameters of this knowledge, bore the sanctified stamps of all pervasive absolutism. The sheens of their activism were well marked in their expertise of the prevalent war games, principled ruler ship, responsible and devoted social beings, temperate habits with no hallucinations etc. They were attuned to clarity of thought and were characteristically wedded to initiatives.

The Indian history is full of examples, that the pillers of Indian culture, as Arjan, Sri Ram Chander, Raja Harish Chander, Udhishter and most of the mystics of medieval age, were the products of such Gurukuls. The teachers of the Gurukuls were held in the high esteems of the Indian thought even now (when the space-age has tapered down the importance of Industrial arena) it stands testified by the fact, that the modern Indian coaches, who succeed in training the younger generation to some eminent discipline, are given an award named after Guru Darona Charya who was regarded as the great trainer of the marshal arts in the Gurukul. His disciples (students) are now being displayed as legendary figures in all compartments of human lives. It therefore stands to reason that the legacy of the Gurukul culture is still occupying the Indian mind-set, though the old order is being tamed out to vacate its abodes to yield its place to new thought. I feel that our culture is blessed with a quality of resilience and can counter to all torques and torsions of the changing times, what-so-ever be the circumstances. It will never go in wilderness, is my firm belief.

The teachers of Gurukuls were accomplished men, and their personalities created an aura, under which their pupils too attained the same qualities in their characters. Our religious preaching have a basic content, which is still repeated in our daily prayers that, "Bharring, a winged insect which has no, off-spring from its own genes, but it is destined by nature, to recreate its species by carrying any alien insect to its abode (which it forms, in some corner of house walls, by majestically erecting a small hump of mud, with one hole for entry and exit) and hatching its all instincts by a constant humming-voice, till that insect takes the form of Bharring itself. The content of this line, a tribute to your guide, as a daily repeated stanza in the morning and evening in certain Mandirs is, "Keet Na Jane Bharring Ko, Guru Kar Le App Smann" that is the alien insect who does not know the Bharring, but it is molded, by his constant humm and motivation, to the very form and characteristics of Bharring itself.

This very principle is applied to the development of the pupil, whose all behavioural and personality traits too, are molded by their motivator, that is their teacher, that was the Gurukul culture.

The Indian society remained under the influence of this culture when the kings like, Chander Gupt Maurya and Ashoka the great, ruled this country. Then it was called a Golden-sparrow, i.e. (the land which produced Gold, diamonds and every other product) and was considered as one of the best land for the sustenance of the early middle age lives. So to say it was a land of abundance and were ruled by the kings, who were culturally superior and brave and were men of principles. They were the protectors of their subjects. It appears that the easy ways of sustainance and pro-people policies of their kings made the Indian people tolerant and slothy.

The traders of other countries who were comparatively much different to us weighed the intricacies and inherent essentials of our social orders, our policies on protectionism, our temperaments, and composures to external out bursts, disposition of our national mind-set, to some erratic behaviour of aliens, our food-habits, our tolerance limits, the intensity of our anger to injustice and also our war games. They obviously served as conduits, to give a back-feed on all aspects of our people and our ways of Governance, with full details of latent and transparent camouflaged reflexes of our Helmsmen. They held an eagle eye over the wealth of this country and prowled the religious and compassionate leaning of our people.

After the advent of the Buddhism and Jainism, which bore the core characteristic of "Ahimsa" (not to injure or kill any being) made our people more vulnerable to be attacked or raided. The avarice of alien culture, to collect maximum material wealth tempted them to loot and murderous assault on our country. Hence the collective wisdom and the exalted, essence of the Indian mysticism, became a major cause of our subjugation to the raiders, from other countries, who were mostly the believers of Islamic way of life. Thus the differentials of graphics, of Hindu and Islamic religions, provided a stepping stone to muscle power to trudge down the subtle and sublimed culture of our country. So after 1000 A.D. our Gurukul culture were opened to abuse and this nursery of subjectivity and mysticism was badly mouled by the alien raiders. Our faith in compassion, mercy, renunciation, discrimination, knowledge, selfless service, lustless love etc. were mocked at, and with that commenced an era of our decline.

As the history stands evidence, that after 1000 A.D. Mahmud Gaznavi a muslim ruler raided and looted our country year after year. He bruised the spirit of Indians, seventeen times. He destroyed the pillers of our culture, as Somnath Mandir and several others sancto-segatious spiritual rudiments of this ancient culture. He removed the Golden idols, studded with diamonds, chandeliers, Golden tombs, butchered our people and even the young men and women were sold in the slave markets of his country. The architectural glory of our civilisation was badly abraised. Then came the Muslim kings who established their own kingdoms in India and ruled this country, in which the spirit of adventurism and initiatives were totally eloped from the psychy of our people.

In the 12th century A.D. Qutabud-Din attacked India and laid the foundations of slave dynasty, which lasted for 300 years. In 1526 AD. Babar, took our the Delhi throne after defeating the then sultan and laid the foundation of Mughal rule. He was a Turk and was a descendent of Mangol leader Changez Khan. The Mughals ruled India upto Aurangzeb.

After about 700 years of Muslim rules there again ushered in an era of self assertion and self-respect and some under currents of Indian self esteem, challenged the autocracy, cruelty and fundamentalism of patronised Islamic culture. Consequent upon which some divinely figures and accomplished men gave their sacrifices to save the remanents of Indianism. Also the young spirit of Indian bravery, inspired the youth to stand as a rock to safeguard their self respect. The case in point is the sacrifice of Guru Teg Bahadur, the power of sword and managerial and psychological skills of Guru Gobind Singh, the war games of Shivaji Marahatta and so many other brave sons of mother India.

In this era of torch and turbulation, there came on Indian scene a class of mercantile interests. They were called, The East India Co. of Britain. They were comparatively better politicians and less brute in nature although they were true to the core in serving the interest of their country. They were past master in their gimmickry attributes and were expert in their judgements. They had studied minutely the prevailing conditions of the Indian sectoral interest and they took up, their own exploits to control this great land, of agricultural and mineral wealth. So after certain war techniques and policy kick backs. The East India Co. led by Robert Clive, took over the virtual rule of Bengal, by winning the battle of Plassy, and laid the deep foot hold to take over the reins of Indian Governance. Rest all is History.

From the above discussion and post-droop study of our culture, my mind is marked with dotted inhibitions, that the main cause of our deterioration was that our nation became so tolerant culturally, and slothy in its actualism, that we could not give even a body blow to the wrong-doer, however big his provocation might be. That our considerate and compassionate vision and our Trance-sublimental-syndromes, made our people coward in the eyes of those, who only understood the language of 'might is right' muscle power and gheto-culture. Moreover our local rulers governed in sectorial divides only, which were riddled with rivalries among themselves. Hence they could not resist the onslaughts, of the outside raiders. Rather they helped the outside attackers to let their own Indian brothers down.

The fact of the history concretise our belief, as we read that when Sikander raided India and king Porass took his challenge and fought bravely, to save the soul of our motherland, his rival king Umbhi, helped the forces of Sikander. Similarly Jai Chand played against Prithvi Raj Chohan. There are several such examples, but my memory is failing to divulge much more, but this behaviour pattern was adopted by many.

Moreover if you just give a cursory look to history of adventurism, during age of Roman Empire and Industrial age that is, from 1000 A.D. to 1925 A.D., there had been at least 29 explorers and adventurers (as per the record of national geographic society) who explored the seas and mapped the Basins of the long rivers, to locate new horizons of the undiscovered lands, and also charted the known and resourceful lands to find the new trade roots for their countries, but there is no mention of any Indian in that category of men, who also might have taken risk to set out on such adventure.

My conscious takes refuge under the deluge of so many dia-tribes, which give an escape rout to my mind only, when I find that almost the whole of the second millennium, i.e. (from 1000 A.D. to 1947), India remained under the foreign rule. The Muslim kings ruled over our country for about 800 years and rest of period the Britishers ruled the roost. Naturally they did not encourage the Indian spirit and talent to be eminently placed in the international contours. The Muslim rulers remained busy in the spread of Islam or loot of the Indian wealth. Consequent upon which, many Indians were converted to Islamic way of life assimilated them in the receptive Indian culture, while they formed the policies and plans, in a way that their own language and culture could foster and progress well in India. As a result of which the old Gurukuls were totally decimated and the whole of our land was punctuated by Madrassas and schools, which were flavoured in Islamic tastes.

When Britishers came and established their rule, they found our culture totally alien to them, and took all our wealth to their own country. It is quite obvious that the soul of Indian culture came under a trudge and the question of adventurism did not arise.

After independence in 1947, the Indian nation started afresh to get our original culture restored, although the cross-sectional fibres were changed in tenor and contents. The original Indians were from Aryan Race, alongwith some ancient tribal sects, but post independence India consisted of Hindus, Muslims, Christians, and adivasies etc. Hence the modern schooling too took drastic changes in its curriculum in history and literature. The medium of instructions were changed to regional and national languages, except, of the courses in mathematics, sciences and technology, as these books could not be available in our national languages. The appreciative epithets for the erstwhile rulers, were changed to national reflexes in tone and textures. The educational courses were oriented to be pro-developmental in core and character. All available excellence and imminence were incorporated by our national Government to help our people, come out of drudgery and droop, ignorance and ignominious dark and draconian awes, and were guided to don the mentles of responsible citizenship.

The prayers in the schools were changed, National Anthem was introduced to inculcate the spirit of nationalism. The script of languages were changed from Urdu to Hindi and other regional languages. The photographs of monarchs and kings were changed, with those of national leaders and freedom fighters. The books of history were rewritten and the heroic deeds of national involvements were eulogised. Even the dress codes were changed. In nutshell all the reflexes of educational centres were changed, within a cushion period, which was necessary to absorb the shocks of a diabatics of changed circumstances.

There was a sudden rise in the developmental activities of the nation. To provide the collosal, manpower, technically trained, and skilled and unskilled labourers for different projects and other allied development works, mushrooms of schools, technical as well as other institutions, health care centres, cooperatives, and all sorts of infrastructures, put our nation on the march. New form of Government on democratic lines, elected by all adult citizens came into existence, which is working according to the constitution adopted by the people of India on 26th of January 1950.

My point of discussion is, the spread of education, its imperatives to meet the new situations, by the architects of this vital input, in the reflexes of the young-scholars, to take up the new challenges, of manifesting a culture of Indianised context, to rekindle and refurbish the old spirit, wedded to old traditions of accomplishments of human personalities were taken up our Government.

For about three decades or so, after our independence, the numbers of schools and colleges increased by many folds, in rural as well as in urban areas, but the excellence and quality of urban based education, remained far better than in the rural areas. Hence the main thrust of qualitative developments, remained the domain of the urbanites, although the well-to-do villagers too enjoyed all opportunities to get their wards, eminently trained in all important disciplines. Undoubtedly, the rural areas too were punctuated with some good schools but the good teachers and professors mostly preferred their placements in the urban areas only. This very practice still prevails, between rural verses urban education. The main impediment of the rural postings are the lack of infrastructural facilities and the non-caring and non-civic, general behavior-pattern of the ruralites.

Both in rural and urban areas, the teacher and taught relationship maintained the legacy of pre-independence environments, but soon after this relationship acquired reversal hysterics, when the steep increase in population growth, created problems of actual unemployment and the job-potential felt out-stripped.

The factors, on which the deterioration of this relationship depended, were the fast and devastating changes in the educational curriculum, which were set in motion to negotiate with the fast moving scientific and technological developments. Because the advent of space-age, needed the high level of capabilities and calibres of teaching community, supported by the necessary infrastructures. But the old techniques and skills, were not phased out and the teaching community too, were not mentally equipped still, to take up the challenges of the fast changing civilization. The result being that there occurred a sort of confusion among the student community, as most of the students who attained a certain qualified level, went in for competitions for government job. Consequently there occurred under currents for cut-throat competitions.

The white-collared job is a legacy of the British rule and the black-hand doctrine which emanates from a work-culture, in which the spirit of practical and pragmatic assertions, glorify the hands, which move on the job, is still a causality in our adoptions, even uptill now when we are ushering in the 21st century. Our people being attuned to, make bucks without any hard labour and not even possessing the level of desired knowledge, are in a mood to grab-rather than to demand it on merits. This tendency has created an undesired and contagious itch, which is hard to handle now with a sense of decency. This syndrome, has mothered an ill-conception, to success, through copying, which has adopted an enormity, of organised methodology. This malady has created a frivolous overtones and has become a bane of modem education. Even the teachers, whom we regard as the nation-builders, do not take risk to discourage this practice, during the conduct of examination, where in the teachers themselves are discharging the duties of supervisions. The common refrain with the students now is to achieve the target by hook or by crook.

The things now stand at such a pass, that if a teacher or an invigilator dissociates with this practice, he is threatened and man handled by students or their sympathiser. Thus this tendency to grab, by deceipt or deception, has so deeply been routed in our system, that the help of police or some other agencies is often taken. There seams to be no end to this dark tunnel. This is a great abuse of our old Gurukul culture.

It is quite obvious the product of this ill-conceived methodology and illegitimate practices, would not stop here only, rather this mode of characterisation would reflect in his future life endeavors as well. If such a person could manage to grab a Government job through the influence of pulls and pressures of his relatives, he may not be faithful in the discharge of his duties. There would be so many cavil or carp against such people. His actions would remain an eye sore to the people, the avarice of such people becomes youthful, even when they grow-old. What our nation can expect from the disciple of such Gurus if he happens to become a teacher? I leave it to be judged by the people.

So with such abuses, the souls of the old Gurus of Gurukuls, would be pulsating to see the deterioration and degradation of their descendants to the lowest ebb. There are schools in the urban areas who are serving the national-cause, the rural education centres however have stooped too low.

On a casual visit to my village, I saw that some teachers indulge in drinking during their duty hours They knew that parents of such and such student do possess the home-distilled-desi-wine, and they got their quota from them. In return, they wood help, their wards in copying in the examination halls. Such exploits of the modern teachers, in the hierarchy of old teachers of Gurukuls, based on selfish thinking of 'I' 'Mine' and 'You' and 'Yours' cannot produce productive or creative talent. Such people with tunnel vision, can only spread an intense fears of darkness in the minds of their pupils who would never be able to accept the harshness and struggle in the future lives.

8

STINK OF POLITICS

Since the times, the social order took the centre stage for maintaining the affairs of the people, for their betterment and for paving the way to a dignified civic order, there rose a necessity for creating certain ways of Governance, which could organise the system with a judicious expediency, in which a man with general prudence could feel a cosy accredition of the managerial skills. The sagacity and perpetualism to manage the affairs of people, needed a class or a party, who could ensure a governance in which the essential inputs would be selflessness, screnity sedateness and servility.

Out of the different ways of Governance, i.e. kingship, autocracy, dictatorship etc. were now out dated. Only the system supported by the voice of the people was sustainable, which had been holding its "Shism", without any cavil and carp, by even the matured and wise people. This system, in one word is "Democracy, that is, the Government of the people, by the people and for the people".

In our country this form of Governance is being run by a multi party system, which incorporates its all available wisdom and maturity to annunciate its plans and programmes, for the benefit of the people who are considered to be the masters to elect the members of the party, whose programmes they find, are beneficial. The elected Government in this way, is meant for a specific time-frame. If it is found lacking in implementing its pro-people programmes, they may be voted out in the next elections.

The spirit of the constitutional law, imbibes in it, that the political parties should select the persons, for fighting the elections, who are men of integrity, selfless service, mentally matured, having a global understanding of worldly affairs, fearless, statesmen like, segacious in planning, honest, upright, truthful, cultured and politically enterprising. The selected persons should adopt a living standard, in which a common man, may identify him as his servant, sympathiser, a sincere guide and a faithful councillor.

My humble but a bit crisp suggestion is that the elected member should adopt, all his postures, as means of transport his dress-code, his eating habits, his daily routine at the same level, as his electorate are routinely maintaining, within the limits of their hard earned money. The simple man with even a tunnel vision, should recognise him as his friend and well wisher. So while living with the people and identifying himself with poorest of the poor, he would get a better feed back, of his electoráte's living conditions and their day-to-day problems at the grassroot level. With this he can better assert while suggesting the pro-people, remedial measures, while discharging his legislation duties. If such a homogeneous attitudes become the common exploits of the elected members, with a sheen of faithful orientations, their people would not suffer from any device of deceptive colouring, and there may appear the reflexes of all smiles.

I have tried to annunciate an ideal pattern, the elected member should own, as a true server. But I am sorry to state the people who stand for elections have a double faceted forms always. You can watch their reflexes before elections and an about-turn change immediately after it. Before elections their availability is more than needed. Even their poses, portends and assumed attitudes are without an arrogance. Their folded hands, with a matching smiles and a small tow-in, of their necks, give every person, a "Yes sir" and "yours own" syndrome and inject in them, a new hope for their aspirations and ambitious demands. Their postures would attain a superfluousness in their assertive semblances and they would try to display their tricks with a fine tuned hypocratic and illusive options. They may enter in the cottage of a poor man, would sit on a old stringed pitted cot, and would not hesitate even to make a show of oneness with the poor, by covering their bodies with dirty quilts, if the weather so permits. Even they may share the meals, or a cup of tea of the poor man. Thus posing themselves to be sentimentally identified with the poor and down trodden. They will try all sorts of other tricks, at his control and commands, to get the votes of such simple and silent people. To accept the courteous calls for joining some function of the poorest man even, and to accept sweet, sour or saltish eatables, would be their priority options. They would change their dress-codes, which may be for election times only. Khadi jackets and Kurta, Pajamas with double or treble pockets, and with an ararotic touch, and pressed with a heavy Iron by some competent dhobi, would be adorned by them, in order to signify their simplistic hysterics, which in the normal course would be their arduous oddity.

Even the female members of the prospective candidates, who otherwise remain a protected commodity and never mix up with the poorly conditioned and hard skinned, hard-working women of the poor people, do come out for their casual mix up and get togetherness with them. The poor, sturdy and neglected women and children would enjoy a heroic look, over the well clad and well-dressed, would be madams. Their persuasive cybers are taken care by the poor women out of pittance, rather than any convincing arguments. They too would opt certain postures to get the votes of such people. The poor persons imbibe in themselves a compassion for these status women simply because they are not shrewed enough to judge their long term strategies.

So all the postures and postulates are the simulations of their hypocratic minds. In heart of heart, they too know that these are the twisted permutations of their compulsions of time. Such cybernetics would be bade good-by, no sooner their purpose is solved.

When the elections are over, the victorious candidates

would be surrounded by his relatives, and sycophants, and the poor voters with whom, he was quite familiar yesterday, becomes an alian and is pushed asides to a "keep-off-distance", from the newly turned-magnimion, whose insulation from their people has now become a combatant necessity. The person who yesterday was taking tea with the poor men with unmeasured quantity of sugar, would sarcastically, say with an eleptical twist on his lingua-franca, "sugar too less, you know, I am a diabetic". Moreover all his reflexes are now found changed to awesome and authoritative tones. The poor people who voted for him, when try to contact him for their problems, he is stated to be busy and having no time to entertain any body. Whatever one has to say, may he given in writing, and be put in a complaint box The methodology adopted is not accountable to any. Thus the voters ultimately feel cheated.

The politicians of modern India are self server, under the guise of patriots The decades of seventies, eighties and nineties have given stories of averice, greed, self assertion, scams and scandals to our people.

We had been hearing in our childhood, our national leaders were busy in fighting with the colonial and imperialist powers, and were exhorting our people to rise from slumber and shred the chains of serfdom and slavery. So far as my memory is helping me in giving out the glimpses of national struggle, it is my projected view that those leaders who lived only for their people were the apostles of peace and angles on earth, who embodied in themselves all qualities of goodness and morality.

I still vividly remember that there were some political conferences in my village in early forties which were witnessed by me in my childhood days. Although my mental horizon and understanding were quite shallow, to judge the complexities and colouring of the dynamics of our freedom struggle, but some of the contents of their speeches and poems of the Gadri-Babas, still echo in my mind. If my memory is not failing me, it was a poem of Baba Wasakha Singh one of the contemporaries of Kama-Gatta-Maru freedom fighters, which was worded as on next page.

(Rag Rang Chhute, Sak-Angg Chhute, Chhutian Wattan Piare Dian Galian Ne, Sewa Desh Te Quam Di Brin Aukhi, Gallan Karnian Buhat Sukhallian Ne)

which meant that, "A desh bhagat (Patriot) is destined to leave his comforts, enjoyments, his relatives and even the streets of his dear land, it is very very difficult and arduous to serve the nation and your country. It can never be the subject of those, who only indulge in loose-talk". Also I had an inkling glimpse in my memory, that one of our freedom fighter had tried to radically define, the personal comfort and needs, with the word, "A desh bhagat, does not have the means at his command, to construct even a kacha hut for his personal use. These were the specifics of our freedom fighters of yesteryears.

Mostly that generation of our leaders, remained in jails in far off, distances from their homes and hearths. 'Kala Pani' was the choicest place in the eyes of imperial controls, for most of them. The erst while kala pani, now has the privileged stature in modern India and is known as Andaman and Nicobar Islands. But the British jailors, could fancy the burning of the fats of our freedom fighter in those jails, such were the turbulators and tortuous gadgets, with which those jails were equipped with.

The father of our nation, Mahatma Gandhi earned his own living to support his family, while fighting for freeing our people from the foreign rule. He earned by farming a three acre piece of farm land in Sabarmati Ashram. He lived in a cottage and used only one bucket of water for domestic purposes. This type of renunciated life was symbolic for demonstrating our leaders to live in similar conditions, as the poorest people of our country live. He even produced his own cloth by spinning his own cotton yarns. His personal needs are not unknown to any body now. So taking cue from him, almost the whole generation of national leaders, followed the same modus operandi. As such all of them religiously followed the code, based on morality and ethics. Not even a single penny they spent from the public contributions. Their mental modules were embedded in statesmanship and betterment of all beings.

The leaders of the above-referred statures, refounded and refurbished the lost glory of our country. Even our mystics, had given us a chequered pattern in our behaviours and beliefs. While going through some scripts, I did learn that Swami Vaveka Nandji, who returned from a tour of U.S.A. and England, with big amount of money, collected for promoting the mission of Param Hans Swami Ram Kishanji, when not elected as a chairman of Belur-Muth-trust, handed over every penny to the elected chairman of the trust and borrowed from him, about 1½ Annas or so, on loan, to cross the Hugli River on boat. Such were the colourings and characters of our religious and political leaders, which have actually been handed over to our modern so-called leaders, in heritage, on which the emblem of our constitution is based on. Even the revolutionaries who believed in tit-for-tat policy, as S. Bhagat Singh, Raj Guru and Sukhdev and leaders of the sorts of Subhas Chander Bose and a number of others who gave their blood for the nation, worked hard to see our people freed from the bondage of slavery and make India a free country, where in the leadership, would guide our nation through their moral characters; which would be on the same lines in attitudes and actions, which had been exercised by their predecessors.

But the history stands dripped, and aghast with a deep sighs of sorrows, to see that the things are not on the same wave-length now. The reversal in the curves of actualism, has created a crisis of character and the things have attained the dimensions which have put our nation to utter darkness. The leadership of the day, stands blinded with averice, egoism greed, self-eulogisation, self-assertion etc. consequent upon this, there seems to be no ray of light. The leadership has masked its face, and the prevailing darkness is not giving any clue to the general public. There is no transparency, and people are exposed to impact of blows in the darkness, as no direction is available. People are standing at a cross, lost in vacuum, and as per version of Mirza Galib are gnawing in their sleeves that,

(Hum Wahan Hain, Jahan Se hum Ko Bhi,

Kujh Hamari, Khabar Nahin Aati)

that is, the poet say, "We are standing on such a cross, where there is darkness around, and we do not know where we are standing".

The political leaders, who had been at the helm of the affairs from late seventies to late nineties had constantly been adopting a reversal postures and had caved in, to the degeneration and denigration of moral values whatever we had received in our heritage from the era of our national struggle, has actually been zeroed by the greedy and gluttonous tendencies of our helmsmen now. The written law and constitutional provisions have been so abused for self-service, that every party is being stamped as stinking and spreading pungent smell. The common man has now imbibed a dotted line version of Governance, that the politics is now a game of crumminious tricks.

The central idea of well-fare state is sub-servient to the welfare of the men in power. Not only the system is now stinking and the dragon of corruption has taken over all of our governing agencies in its jaws, rather the whole phenomenon has opted to an unprincipled adaptations. The common man is so baffled that even the empiricals of the leacherous tendencies are not being understood. The cross-talk of the men in streets, is that, they are ready to assimilate these unethical practices even, but the players who are responsible for this deluge, should have some principles. This idea emanating from the compelling circumstances has been well expressed by some Urdu composer as under:

(Bahar Ho Ke Khazan Hum Guzar Lein Lekin

Yahan Tow Aehley Chaman Ka Kio Asule Nahin)

the poet says, that "People can pass there time in poverty even, without any arrogance, subject to the condition that the people who count in governance and authority should have some principle".

We daily study the newspaper, head lined with stories of scam and scandles of political masters, who had been responsible for managing our affairs. They had gone whole hog, for the mercenary gains. Even their relatives and family members did not hesitate to exercise their unconstitutional skills to tilt the balances of the Government agencies in favour of themselves or their own hench men. Thus the funds allotted for the benefit of the people in general are pocketed by a few privileged. Even the politicians who take oath to remain faithful to the constitution, while exercising their powers of judicious expediencies in implementing Government plans, not only misuse their constitutional oaths but also abuse the spirit of judicious incorporations by allotting the purchase, procurement and constructional works to their favourites for a consideration. Thus such practices which are detrimental to the national interests are encouraged and get a boost under the official partnership rest of things are then taken care of, by the investigating agencies, courts and information medias.

The twists and turns of the law and legal luminaries scribbling with the senses and similes of the legal supplements and judgment, now become the rejoinders and refurbishments catalytics, for taking refuge for a cushioned time frame. Such complex battles then go on for a longtime and the impacts and impulses of such illegal manoeauvres, is lost thin in the minds of the people. The wrongdoer again works out his dynamics, and present himself as a victim of the circumstances and certain inviduous invectives from his rivals. His consciousness, may be giving his mind a rebuff for his hypocratic behaviour but who cares?

This treachery has not remained the domain of our politicians only, rather this contiguous disease has gone down to officialdom, right upto the level of the lowly placed employee. The electronic media and newspapers, have further helped in publicising these scandalous derivatives, as a result, the general health of our governing bodies and beauracracy has totally become immune to all sorts of criticism. The common numerator for this immunity, is the habit of our people, to link such hypocracy to be affected by space of time, to the graphics of their memories, and to lend credibility to the short termed promises at the time of elections again.

The things have been stooped so low, that even the panchayat elections of villages, are fought with this idea that who-so-ever would be elected a member, he and his relatives would get a new avenue for earning some extra money. So the whole system from minister, beauracrats, clerks, peons to panchayats, is stinking and has been totally venomised by the bug of corruption.

Leave aside the political set ups, even the religious bodies and trusts are not free from this disease. Even there, the people are seen quarreling and using intolerable invectives against each other. Where is then, the scope of service, to which every body is supposed to be wedded.

The written laws are all ethical, but on papers only. In practice every law is being abused by its protectors. It may be the law of any "ism". The only detterent and safeguard to this can be the level of wisdom of an individual, otherwise the end of the tunnel is still far off. An individual cannot see his character in the mirror, it can be gauged only by the voice of people. A society which loses its moral values, is destined to droop and degradation. If we do not rectify and reform our behaviour, the new generation will sarcastically stair at us.

One more major drawback in our way of Governance is, that the leaders of the day have developed an aptitude, to install their own sons and daughters, in the political hierarchy. Their only qualification is that their father is confronted with the adversities of this line. In almost all the states, the ministers are busy in establishing their off springs, rather than to look to the well-fare of the people on priority These minions work as de-facto ministers in the areas of influence of their fathers. All departmental officialdom, which deals with the general public, is instructed to obey to the dictates of minister's sons & daughters. Such extra constitutional power make the system work in accentricity to their normal trajectories, where so many ifs and buts emerge out and the whole fabric of the state-power is put to undesired stresses. The person in the scene being not accountable to any misdemeanours, the department concerned bears the responsibility of all the stink which ultimately pollutes the minds of the people and put the system to disrepute. This practice has become a copy book way to politics these days, and younger generation of the leaders find an automatic and ready made conferment to walk in the foot prints of their fathers. This *modus operandi* is a source of heart-burn, amongst those who are not so resourceful, but are far-better qualified and skilled, as compared to the lolly-pop off-springs of these modern leaders. So the stink of politics gets incremented to create mental pollution in the minds of the people.

The big-wigs in politics have attained such an intemperate behaviours that the advices, imparted by them through the blares of loud speakers, for the digestion of general public, are rendered meaningless, when their own actualism is displayed as a contemptuous infringements of the rules and regulations of the departments. It is often seen that the leaders of national and state level set-ups, when allotted the Government houses, use them and make amendments and alterations in their structures in contravention to the prevailing laws. They do not hesitate even to encroach upon the public lands. They forget about the span of time, they are tenured to stay in those residences rather they try to push that period, by lame excuses and self-made compulsions, to make those Government estates their permanent fieldoms. The authorities concerned are compelled to serve them with legal notices, which are also reflected through the public medias, to which the people react in sarcastic tones. Thus there ushers in, a public debate, with caustic epithets, which make such leaders to be found in the lowest echelons of the public mind-sets, which ultimately put their reputation to an abyssimal depths, the recuperation of which may even go to desperate reversals, wherefrom they need certain special re-suscitation drills to get to the rails for their normal activity. So such torsional pressures on their intelligence modules, make them to do some rethinking to refurblish their orientations and make them behave. This duress-prone dynamism has become a common refrain of the modern politicians.

Such pavilious omissions and commissions find their place through the pervious layers of officialdom also from top to bottom, and also the party cadres who rule the roost, adopt the same very activism from top to grass-root level worker. The simple analogy followed by the wrong doers is that if the higher planes, do not allow any inclination in this syndrome, why the small fries are asked to shed their invectives. This mental malfunction, thus goes unchecked these days. This whole phenomena has increased the level of further stinks in the already polluted mind of our modern politics which is leading us to wrong paths.

9

OLD VS. NEW GENERATION

A major source of tension in our domestic lives is the relations between the young and old. The gap in age has a direct bearing on the thinking, maturity wisdom, domestic vibes, sensual desires, food-habits, likes and dislikes, sense of discrimination, a feeling of responsibility, renunciation and so many abstract feelings, which one encounters in one's daily routine. All these traits are tizzy and deeply prick one's temporal attributes, but remain latently embedded in the layers of one's covetous actualism. This sort of suppression of one's feelings. I presume, is the major input ingredient, for opening up, one's metabolism to so many complex health syndromes, which ultimately mothers the diseases as heart-infarction, blood pressure, paralysis, diabetes, loss of memory, loss of vision, orthopaedics and so many other health problems. This, then becomes a major source of disturbance and distress, in the family set-up.

The major under current, in the hallucination of environments, is the abuse of emotional attachment, which the old people think, as a direct robbery on their sentimental cartels, which they presume as their monopoly. Their presumptive right, may not be in right direction, but the old-thought catapults it, to the maximum stretch, and feels badly mould when the tension in the strings is suddenly released. The compulsions of the times, and the imperatives of the children are totally changed, as the younger generation too, have a right to be placed in the proper slot of love and affection, to be as nearer to the radical assertions and realism of life, as possible. They too need a freedom to lead their lives, comparably to match their age limits and the compatibility of their understanding and exact comprehensions of their minds, to create harmony and mutual respects, in the terro-technology of their future life graphics. For that matter the old generation should not interfere in their routine, rather they should be helped financially and advised only where they need it, otherwise it would be an encroachment on their thinking. The old people must look to their own past about 30 years back, when they too were young, the mother-in-law was also an obedient Bahu.

So far as the sentimental feelings are concerned, the orbits and trajectories are the same in all young-ages. There may be some difference in magnitudes and modus in the individual young lives, but the level of sublimed sentimental feelings are more or less the same. The only difference is that, the level of wisdom gained through one's experience, for which only the old generation is the gainer, but the point they ignore is, to properly screen their own past. If probed they would consciously feel, that their youth was more defiant, than their off springs now. The old generation actually bears sarcasticism for the issues, which they themselves have gone through, so the tension existing in the families, are partly the outcome of ignored analyticals of actualism and normal flow of individual aptitudes and interests. This aspect of joint family system needs the catalytic incorporation of one's experiences, which naturally becomes the prerogative of the old people.

However there are certain aspects which are to be looked after and taken care of by the young ones only. They should not forget that their place and slots in the societical contours are the results of sacrifices of their elders. Their faces which they see in the mirrors are the graphics and blue prints of their parents, which stand testimony to their descendence in the family-tree. When the younger generation goes oblivious and invidious to their elders. The old parents feel cheated and their state of mind become an analogous to that of a tree, which stands isolated in the jungle in autumn season. All its leaves and fructifying-tendings, having got lost, its ecological simmerings, loose, to make the nature more purifying and fresher. Such a tree stands in solitude, and no living being is ever attracted towards it. Similar becomes the condition of old people, whose sons under certain eccentric consideration loose interest in the parents. There are a good number of such people also, which we do come across in our daily lives.

My attention goes a bit observatory when I come across certain sign-boards bearing the words in capital letters, as, "SENIOR CITIZENS HOME". My curiosity also grows to interact and have a cross talk with these people and assess about the circumstances under which they have left their homes and hearths, in the twin-light years of their age. The reasons gathered are many, but in the 95% cases, the episodes start after the marriages of their male children. After their marriages, the sons mostly become pro-in-laws, and the major factor is their wives, while daughters go pro-parents and the major partners are their in-laws.

This is the vital juncture where the family relations do get a sharp turn and the mental balance of family members comes under strain.

As already discussed above that about 5% families may be fortunate enough, where the conditions are satisfactory and without tension, but mostly the joint families remain under different curvatures of strain. I shall now try to discuss the reasons to which these strains and stresses may be attributed to, in our social lives.

1. It has been observed that if the parents are having more than one son and the sources of income are limited, all the sons would try to extract as much money from their parents as they possibly can. Even the brothers do not see eye to eye with each other. The poor old frames, are put to so much pressure that they very often are dangerously placed and are rendered penniless. If the sons have a bit of sympathy for their parents, their counter parts do poise against their in-laws, to an extent that the husbands are instigated to the level that they do begin behaving invectuously with their parents and in some cases even the physical fiddles do take place and the old souls are shown the exit ot the house. In such cases the old parents

are left to fend for themselves. They are found, taking refuge in some religio-social institution or with some of their relative, who may be having some sympathy with them.

2. In some cases the in-laws of the sons, do play a most criminal part, in making the lives of the old parents, a den of hell. They would try to get their son-in-law, work, to their dictates, and would create conditions through the manovourings of an obnoxious behavior of their daughter that old parents of the boy are totally lost in vacuum and their minds are put under so much strains and turbulations that their physical condition go totally deplorable. Their health runs down and become prone to all sorts of complexities of health syndromes. They are compelled to get themselves adjusted under some alternate arrangements. Such cybernetics exercised by the in-laws of the boy, cover in their ambits all the sources of his money-flows even, so as to make their domestics, work in tune to the whims and fancies of their daughter, which may bear the orientations of servitudes to her whole family. Such people are crooks of superlative degrees, whose only aim is self assertion and to present themselves, with topsy-turvy and hypocratic talks before the people.

3. The marriages of sons and daughters, which are arranged these days, are done, without knowing much about the hidden traits of the two families, which often becomes the subject of possibilities of adjustments later on. Sometimes one has to adjust with a defiant and delirious counter-part about whom, the other family comes to know after the marriage. The whole terro-technology of the family set up is disturbed and fills with tension. The old parents of the boy are not even shown the formal gestures, which they expect as a customary regards, from their daughter-in-law. Rather her defiant attitude keep the old souls, showered with a caustic radiation's from her constellative aura, and their dying instincts are further mystified for being surrounded by a canopy of cold and non-receptive attitudinal reflexes. The daughter-in-laws never consults her in-laws for any exchange of social-pleasantries, neither they are asked regarding the choices of their eating habits. Her reflections in the routine house-hold are always unidirectional. All big and small. Who-so-ever enters the house would be her defacto-right

to deal with, even if the old in-laws, would be sitting in one corner of the house. From birth to death all types of ceremonies would be covered under her prerogatives only. It would be considered infructuous and incomplete without her. However superfluous the whole affair may look but her own instincts would be satisfied only if she could attract the attention of all and sundry. Even if somebody would have the wisdom to ask her about the non-presence of any elder, on certain occasion, she would reply through an elliptical cones of her mind to taper the whole affair to look justifiable.

Even the consellers of such unconventional ladies, would be some ones who are equipped with a torpic-in-phobe mentality, who know the weakness and egoism of such person. By mere some huffs and puffs, which suit to the temperaments of such house-holds ladies they get their own interests served even by getting strings of her purse loosened. Such acrobats and exposures are misunderstood as social adjustments, rather than an exercise towards a catalytic stupidity. So whosoever knows the catapults of the prevailing environments of such houses, would go straight to the house hold lady, would chat, talk and satisfy his/her pooh-bah ambitions and walk away, while the old-in-laws would sit mute and mouled in some corner of the house, and would helplessly watch their own house being burgled. Even some of such visitors would not-hesitate to pass some obnoxious remarks against the old parents of the boy, to win favour of the invidious house-lady, who now is recognised as an extravagant incumbent to serve their self seeking attributes. The old and out dated human configurations, would simply feel the pinch of a momentary slip, which had made them repent and would keep them tensile till the end of their lives.

One thing which may come in one's mind is, why no son, even takes the side of his parents? It can only be said that, these are the times of predominance. No considerate and wise person would try to expose one's own belly to any one. If dominance takes on to dominance the family's equation is badly disturbed, and some catastrophic developments may also take place. Hence the sons too have no other choice than to flow with the tide and their tolerance cushion becomes a bit wide and it works to the detriments of the old parents only. The compulsions of the time, therefore, make the old lot as their first causality and the trauma of tensions and turbulations goes on:

4. I have come to learn, from the cross-talks of certain senior citizens, that certain families who are quite sound economically and lead luxurious and ultramodern lives, are one step ahead of others. They hesitate to see their old parents, and never come to their rooms even for formality sake. In case of illness the old parents would do their all odd jobs, as washing, stitching, bathing, cleanings, by themselves. If some body in the family shows some sympathy, he will arrange some servant for the old parents, who may help them in their routine endeavors, in a mechanical pattern, but where would be an emotional touch, which every old couple wants to enjoy? The servant or maid can do some cursory jobs and would collect their wages. If the old parent is chronically ill and he/she cannot attend to his/her personal hygiene, only some member of the family who is emotionally attached to them, can do it, not a paid servant. So in case, the son/daughter do not show any emotional attachment with their parents, the doom looms large and only the God could be graceful to give them strength and vigour to pass their troubled times. It is my general experience that under such conditions the daughters are comparatively, more sympathetic and service prone to their parents than the boys. In case, non of the blood-relation takes any interest in their old parents, then my mind feels locked to look beyond this tunnel.

5. In case of two or more sons, having their families and children, but with meagre-income, the old parents are always under tension to see their off-springs in hardship. In case they help a bit, who is comparatively scantly placed the others would raise a hara-kiri, thus the lives of the old parents would be made a hell. In villages where the people are not markedly educated the disputes amongst mothers-in-laws and daughters-in-laws, would emerge even if the mother-in-law, takes in her lap the weeping child of the other daughter-in-law, after dropping the one belonging to her. In such houses also the old people are not taken care of at all and are often considered as a scrap commodities.

It is a credentially accepted conclusion in our culture that the old people are at the mercy of the daughters-in-law. Some may have an element of compassion or wisdom, while others may not have such ingredients, which are an important input to place the old people of the family in a respectful slot, the son's generally keep themselves astray and play only a second fiddle.

I do not take this as an ever existing dotted-line behavior in all families, rather there are a few, whose sons are dominant and they do not tolerate even a grain of disrespect or disregard to their old parents, but that number is quite small. Mostly the parents of the boy are sufferers and feel robbed off and cheated.

So much so, is the level of ignoring the old people, that even they are not congratulated on the birth-days parties of their son, which are often held in the houses of the urbanites. I have observed that son himself or his wife would always be in the fore-front to receive the congratulatory gestures in person or through phone calls. No body bothers about the persons, who gave birth to the birthday baby and sacrificed their every thing on the development and education of their ward. The old souls in their twil-light years, would see, their yearning for affection for their son, stand muzzled and trudged by an unresponsive and non-receptive stoics of the circumstances. This sarcastic attitude would tinker the mind of old and helpless mother, who would take protection under the drips of her eyes, to soothe her burning instincts, and would work out a compromise between the logistics and legacies of motherhood, with a natural dictum, that what benediction she had played to her son, if she kept him in her womb for nine months? After all it was her compulsions to become a mother.

One thing which should be crystal clear to all concerned. that the time gap get such a treatment is never more than thirty years, when these masters of the present, would themselves slip into that slot, and they may also receive the same treatment. Their past may then stair at them satirically with their egos and assertions now gone in reversals and reciprocity in the actualism of their life cycle. Their attitudinal adaptations in the young age, have already carved out the same type of characteristics in the cerebral frames of their children. The times have stood evidence, when the knots tightened by hands in self assertions and self-eulogisation, would have to be opened by your teeth, when all your faculties having gone weak, no tonic would come to your help to pull you out from the deluge of self-deceit. You can simply glance at your past behaviour, to meekly submit to your consciousness and repent on your follies of youth. Only then the oft-repeated epithet used by you for the old parents is religiously understood. Which were worded as "So what, if you have done for your son, every body does it". The hard fact of life is that, "Only one whose house is burning feels that he is being destroyed, otherwise the people see in it, an incarnation of Agni Dev". This is a straight derivation of life realism.

I am not wise enough to impart any advice to my old brothers and sisters, but one thing which gives some consolation to my own mind is to always see towards deficient and deprived people and thank God for, still being benevolent to you. Secondly let us all learn to adjust as far as possible and never be demanding from off-springs. If they do not have a civic sense of wishing you well, while going out and do not have even a dinghy habit to ask you, your taste, do not have a courtsy of enquiring of your feelings and your conditions in case of disease etc. Never demand it and keep your cool. Pass your time in religious studies and witness the young people playing games etc. It will reduce your gloom and boost your spirit don't try to discuss your demeanours with all and sundry as this creates an extra tension on your mind. Pass on time in studying the nature and religious scripts only. If possible don't have any ill will against any, as it exposes you to so many health hazards. If possible pay a visit to a reputed hospital emergency. You would get morally stronger. Be simple, serene and sedate but not stupid-keep your eyes wide open and keep away from the company of self-server. If your tendencies and interests do not clash, try to visit some saintly figures and discuss with him, the dynamics of your inner consciousness. Trust in God, do good and do not expect any thing in lieu of it.

From the above discussion, I have tried to express my views, based on my personal experiences. The abstract of this discussion lead us to assess, the degree of pollution, which our mental digestion has assimilated in our general behavior to the roots and stems of our family tree. This pollution also creates conditions, for physical degeneration of our elders. The times have so changed, that our old, culture has totally been covered by the hi-fi's of modern times. The old people who were respected and regarded religiously in Hindu way of life, now only receive a hybrid-hackles The pious and pure submission to the sublimed and subtle subjectivity by touch of the feet of elders are now a defiant characteristic of the new generation. The purity of your submission has now been elbowed out by a 'Hallo-Hi' gestures, which have polluted the modern-mind to the extent, that to get an 'ashirvad' from your elders which was an automatic derivation of the 'piey lagun' actualism, has now been subjugated to an unethical modernism. These twists and torques have put our social struts, to rust and redundance. I fear that our culture would be rendered alien and out moded, if we did not stop copying the hollowed and base less ultra-modernism.

10

STINK OF OFFICIALDOM

The officialdom these days, is an integrated network of some persons, who are so-called public servants, which in real well fare states are for the well fare of the people. As per the rules and regulations and the written manuals, they are to help the people to encourage them in their day-to-day, accentuations of civil orders and also promote their interests in entrepreneurship, by guiding them to channelise their energies and genius to build up the infrastructure and boost up the national wealth, by producing more and more qualitative consumer goods, agricultural and acquarian products. In simple language, they are termed servants of the people. As the meaning of the word servant goes, a man of ordinary prudence even, knows that it meant a person who would remain at the beck and call of his master. Of course 'Master', is too harsh a word in its verbitism and actualism, but we may give it a milder tone and may say that a person who looks after the interests of his master without any hesitation and without caring much for his own comforts, may be termed as the servant. Actually the working for the interest of some individual on getting the cost of one's labour should be defined in some other way, rather than being called a servant. The more suitable word to a hireling in lieu of his wages should be termed a "Worker" instead of a servant. As the service is a nomenclature which should be predicated with the word "selfless". As a thumb rule, only the mother is defined as doing a service for her child, who does everything for her baby but without any ambition or desire. But here the so called servants of the people, who have over-stripped the corridors of the Government offices are all for "Selfish" ends only and do not graduate to be called the public servants.

When the nation is on the march and its economy is in the process of development so many arterial and allied channels come into existence, which are constantly working for adding to the gross national production and give a boost to the national coffers fill-ups. So to say, that every able citizen of the country is engaged in doing some productive work, for which the government of the time creates certain infrastructures to help the people in regulating and channelising their energies in proper directions, of which the persons maintaining the different departments, are the vital links between the people and their well fare nodes. They have been recruited to guide those who are not even in a position to fairly explain their own problems, and do need the help of the departmental men to get their points and problems to be brought under the purview of the Government schemes. But their misfortune is that they are exploited by the same very people who are paid by them. That is the turn, where the word "servant" stands in self-diciet.

The mind-set of the officialdom is not pro-people rather the menace of corrupt practices have put the people's faith in the bureaucracy and babudom in a very very bad taste. I personally feel that even an educated person, goes sarcastic and stoic, if he has to get even a minor work cleared from some office Babu. It may be easier sometime to approach the person in higher echelon but to get the file moved from lowest level is an arduous job. As is prevalent in the Indian system, all the initiative for action starts from the lowest rung officials, to which the common man has to encounter. Whatever safeguards may be publicised and propagated regarding the streamlining of the rotten and moth-eaten system, to avoid delays in the disposal of cases, supported by single-window clearance instructions etc. but the mind-set of the babudom is so attuned, that it would not shed its habitual lithargic ness and their inherent unresponsive syndromes. I have heard the officials at the lower rung, saying that to get their importance felt, they should make the client, pay maximum visits to the office, and the clerk concerned should get all his personal interests served to his entire satisfaction. Now any body can judge as to what extent the incumbent baboo, may droop to satisfy his whims, which is his sole discretion to get the poor client plummeted in satisfying the averice of a public servant. The things have drooped so low, these days that this loot is daily going on, right under the nose of the competent officers, who do not dare at all to intervene or enquire, as to why so much delay is going on for even a very very minor work. The dynamics, of these practices are not difficult to understand that the loot is shared by all and sundry.

You may go for getting the license of a scooter, for preparing a ration card, getting the date of birth of your child registered, getting your vehicle registered, getting a mutation deed done or other minor job done. The clerk concerned would see towards you with lulled eyes, and would speak to you with a typical-nodal-pressure, on his throat, as if to convey to you the commands and controls his seat is destined with. He would treat you as a prey, which himself has walked into the den of a man eater. You will have to shell out a hefty sum from your pocket, which your so called servant would convey to you through his symbolised proverbs.

A person whose house is burgled would get an FIR registered after a gruelling kow-tow of the police officials which is merely a formality as I have not heard that a poor and unresourceful man, ever has got his stolen material recovered. You go for getting your power supply restored, your telephone line got rectified, your water supply and sewerage mechanism got rectified, you will feel the pinch when every attendant of the fault would demand something from you. This stage would also come after two, three days space of time, from actual registration of complaint, that too when you have made solid efforts to contact all pillers and posts severally. Such are the environments prevailing in the Government departments, for getting your petty jobs done.

In case you have to get some job done for establishing your business and some financial institutions are involved, you have to cross the corridors of ministers in charge and high level bureaucrats. The Trauma you exercise and the middle men loot, to which you cannot by-pass at all, is indescribable and only the person who experiences it can feel the predicament.

The public postures of high ups in officialdom are for publicity only. The real actualism is impregnated with unresponsive, uncalled for, unprincipled and unhelpful mentality, which works more towards the retardation rather than acceleration of the entrepreneurship, in new initiatives and innovations, to help promote the new avenues for the progress of the country. The babudom whom the people have given employment to help maintain the system, is stinking with a complex syndrome of self service. The common man's basic consideration these days is, that it is only the money which makes the mare go. A person with weak financial position but having all other ingredients as inputs, to in corporate his thoughts in productive schemes and projects, has to encounter all sorts of complex and complicated 'ifs' and 'buts', of the officialdom untill and unless he manages to shell out hefty sum to get his scheme through. If an ordinary person incorporates his energies and initiative after squeezing out all his means, gets to install some technical project in small scale, the baboodom and inspection, agencies of some two dozens departments begin prowling his works every month and would display their authority to harass him, under the pretext of the deficient provisions in his environments, which according to them are contravening the law. But when they get their palms greased, all the rules and regulations automatically fit in the prevailing infrastructure of the project. This sort of practice is never stopped and goes on unchecked whatever little the person earns through his initiative and hard labour is regularly extracted, by these faithfuls of the departments. This is normally termed as the "monthly being paid". These illegal and illegitimate practices are known to all high up, but as the booty is shared by all, this stink never sees its end.

The officialdom is only helpful to those who belong to political party in power, that is the people who are at the helms of the affairs. For them all the rules and regulations are helpful and all discretions of bureaucracy are at their beck and call. They are not even troubled to get out of their cosy drawing rooms, and all the formalities of the provisions of law are complied with, by the officials themselves even without the knowledge of these people. They do not even know as to what were the deficiencies in their project plans, and what precautions and safeguards they are to observe in prospective, so where the Peters are harrassed, the Pauls are unnecessarily favoured. These are the outline behavior of the modern governance.

From small and petty work to bigger projects, the people in general have a rhetoric and a sarcastic perception that the mechanism of official pavlovianism, steered by the cold cynicism of Government officials, makes the things so jittery and time consuming, that the person feels totally fatigued and feverish, uptill the time, some light becomes visible, out of this tunnel. The person generally gets all his sources of sustenance exhausted and feels that how futile and arrogant is the camouflage of the official dynamism, protected by the cybernetics of the law, which queers the pitch of so many twists and turns for the common citizens, while the avericial and gluttonous arterials of Governance go on, with their treacherous-terro-technology, bearing the reflexes of jackish-smiles, at the cost of deeply-felt-rhythmic sighs, of the people. The pollution of the system has got such a potential now, that any further buckling, would up root, all the struts and columns, if some, sanity does not intervene even at this late stage.

Regarding solid working hours of the babudom less said is better. The way these people are working and the safeguards of their rights, who are well protected under the law and the politically backed unionism only speak for their right. No body ever bothers about their responsibilities. If some honest or upright, officer ever points out their deficient work culture, an unnecessary controversy is created which very often stems in agitational attitude and practical demonstrations take place, official work is obstructed and even the concerned officer and his family members harassed and meet with obnoxious epithets and abusive language. In that case even the commands and controls in the higher level do not support the harrassed officers openly, but sheepishly would pass on their time tested imperatives, in a lighter vain, that, "Please deal with these people tactfully". So the system has been badly affected and tended towards in efficiency and lethargy. The official mind set has been obsessed to get benefits without any work.

So far as the working days in a year are concerned, the Government employees who are the initial movers and are the watch dogs for the Government schemes, are enjoying the privileges of closed days in offices, which approximately workout to be 180 days, out of the 365 days of the year. These days also include the national holidays, when all the employees are supposed to attend the national functions, but no body bothers about such sentimental issues. Even the condolence meetings are ignored and all the holidays are enjoyed by them in their own ways alongwith their families. Obviously ½ a year is supposed to be as the working period. But the work culture of the officialdom again puts a big question mark to work out the actual men for which these people do sit in their seats.

The common refrain of officialdom is to play truancy and proxy absenteeism. It has been experienced that whenever a person goes to an office of some Government department, to get an information for one's already pending job, the immediate response would be that the clerk concerned is on leave and no other man can respond to your enquiries. If you have the chance to meet some other sufferer like you, and he would be generous enough to tell you that he had been informed by some official that the baboo sahib is on short leave, which means that the concerned baboo has left a note, for being away for two hours, without mentioning the time of his departure. So whatever may be the time instant, the reply would be the same, and that two hours short leave, would take in its embrace the full-day, duty span. Two or three persons whom you might see, the ladies employees would be found chatting amongst themselves and doing some knitting work. They may be doing something but not their duty, others two males you would be informed as having gone out for taking tea at an outside tea-stall. So virtually the whole lot would be absent or truant. If the public pressure is so great and rush of the people collected raises the fear of raising a Hara Kiri in that case, you may find that some fingers are moving on the papers. Or if the duties are so pro-customer, as the collections of electricity bills, water bills, or bank transaction etc., where in long queues of the people would not allow them to be negligent, the employees would be found working, otherwise the willing reflexes of performing one's duties are few and far between.

Even the officer in charge, would mostly be found out of his office, on tour or on site etc. If ever he is found and informed about the prevailing situation, he will simply while away the predicaments of the people, by certain oblique and oblivious reasoning which would reflect his own compulsions and helplessness. So under the explained environs as above, whom the poor sufferers should see. The system has gone so much bankrupt that no body has got any sense towards their responsibility and predicaments of the people.

On many occasion, the official leave patron happens to be holidays for full five days of the weak, and on the next working day, the people do get the same preface, of truancy and lethargy. The faith of the people therefore stands totally shattered. The poor sufferers would now try to find certain short cuts to get their jobs done, through some middle man, who would become a conduit to get his job done, after certain consideration. This will help you to find some breathing space for your sustenance.

There were certain Government or semi-Government departments, which had got reservation for new recruitments for the wards of their officials. Consequent upon which all the lolly-pops and bullu-dulloos who were not capable of competing any examinations became the privileged guests in the corridors of the Government. The privilege were mainly utilized by the employees, who worked in the Head offices and who were the very operators of this dynamism. The result was that the power centres became the fiefdom of the Head office baboos and officials, and there came a sort of family rule in certain departments. The tiffins they carried, became multi-potted and spacious. Some offices were such in which four to five people of the same family were posted, there by making the things worse for the people, as the truancy, absenteeism kik-backs, hindrance and heckling etc. became a common denominator and every body worked as per the guidance and dictates of the senior member, while the public was put to more and more embarrassment. The whole family would bring their lunch in two big tiffins and one of the member would always come late for two hours or so, as he had to carry the lunch boxes from the house. No body would check such nefarious practices of such people as the senior member of this fiefdom would be clever enough to in corporate all his skills in sycophancy and faithfulness to the chair of that section. Now probably this reservation policy has gone haywire, but the opportunity availed during those days. Are still controlling the cyber-sensitivities of certain sections of the power corridors.

Such recruitments made by the departments were so exploited by certain people, that they cleverly got one or two seats for the members of their families or their near relatives every year, and now the same people who were without any talent were dictating their ways, through their wrong-headed notions, in which they have been well trained by their senior family members. No aesthetics and ethics, are their domain, except, an illegal extraction of benefits from all sources, which come their way. This malady has become a galloping uglification in the complex actualism of the Government departments.

In addition to this loot, such people also put the Government exchequers poor by crores, by claiming bogus medical bills, and certain routine maintenance hand receipts. Certain group of employees with some rapport with the chair, pool themselves to swallow the whole budgetary, allotments, amongst themselves while the deserving employees never get a single-penny, as the claims of deserving employees are tethered in bits and are lost in the dealing hands, as there is no accountability for such lapses.

The *modus operandi* of such officials had been that they drew every day the bogus medical claim, to the extent, the section controlling officer had the power to disburse. If the officer incharge has got the power to disburse Rs. 50.00 in one go, the baboos of the section, would draw Rs. 49.95 daily, as a medical claim in connivance with some government dispensary doctor, who would receive certain percentage as his share. The official would of course be generous enough to leave Rs. 0.05 with the Government coffer, as a token symbol of their being justified and over-cautious to be objected to, by some later on audit etc. This was the only work which was not delayed and was done regularly by the baboos, there used to be a queue every day of employees to collect their bogus medical claims. Some baboos have shelled out so much money that they had constructed big houses and acquired some other properties.

Thank God that some better counsels prevailed upon, and the Government has fixed the medical allowance to Rs. 250.00 only, except of course for some indoor patients in some reputed hospital, which can be disbursed. Of course these people are now raising a hue and cry, and finding fault with this safeguard taken by the Government.

The ugliness and stink of the polluting system, have now crossed all limits. The pavlovian reflexes of the public are being so re-oriented, against the officialdom. That some sort of storm is in the offing, which would become historic catastrophy to be remembered by our future generation, that this type of cold cynicism and unbridled officialdom had struck our nation in the past.

11

INTOLERANCE

It sprouts from the demonic reflexes of the lower mind. It can be compartmentalised in social, political, ethical and religious graphics of the societical chess. Whatever may be its cause, the effects would remain the same, that is, rage, cruelty, riots, destructions, wars, hatred, discrimination etc. are the fruits of the tree manured by intolerance.

This trait in the life characteristic of human being, is directly applicable numerator in the complex combinations of the actualism of life curves, take a man more and more away from the conscious absolute and from eternal bliss. It brings a person under a deluge of rage, wrong headed notions, jealousy, and covers his thinking devices under the foggy layers of confusion and bewilderment. His behavior adopts dangerous postures and his energy channels are, menacingly misdirected towards some misconceptions of civic behavior. The result being, that he may land himself as well as people around him, to some catastrophic trouble spots, which may prove disastrous to the whole family or even to society as a whole.

The most dangerously placed intolerance spectrum is the religious intolerance. Our being a multi religious society, the scope of this dragon, to make its presence felt is much more. We do study in newspapers and also hear and watch in radios and TV networks, that there are pretty good numbers of religious disputes. The core problem for such disputes is that the majority of the people do fall a prey to the propagation and publicity of the religious fundamentalists, who do not recognise the basic principles of existence, rather they spread a venoum to brand the practitioners of other faiths as infidels. They do, form public processions and begin raising slogans and using derogatory remarks against the other religions. Consequent upon this intolerance, there occur religious disputes which even take the form of communal riots. The ignorant and illiterate people, are destroyed and killed, while the perpetrators come out harmless, even after their preposterous activities.

A peep into our historical past stands evidence for the invidious imprints on our culture, under the garb of observing devoutness in a particular faith. There had been so many clashes, encounters, unjust killings, reactions, abrasions to truthfulness and sanity, divisions and demarcations of new areas, wars and all sorts of human sufferings. Mostly the faith of rulers were given official protection and followers of other faiths, were put to severe torches and were also sacrificed at the alter of various edicts or religious indictments by the so called ritualists of the Governing faith. However true and pious, in practice and percepts, the practitioners of other faiths be. The blinded eyes of the Governing faith could not come out of their tunnel vision. Even in day-to-day life of society, we daily see that this religious intolerance, do create conditions which become the routine cause of communal tension amongst different sections of the nation, resulting in an eruption of communal riots.

The religious intolerance is so intense, that even the people practicing the same faith, are compartmentalised in different ethnic groups, which becomes the cause of sustained tension amongst different sects. The people are put to unnecessary disputatious stares and satires, which is continued from generation to generation. This religiously catalysed misconception of thinking, goes so blind that it rarely hears or attend to any reason or logic. History is full of so many examples, when even the great scientist and seekers of truth, were sacrificed and torchered at the alters of blind faiths, even after they had verified the undiscovered knowledge and verified it, through scientific experiments. The blind-priest-hood and religious bigotry of the time, muzzled down the substantiated reality and went to the extent of burning down all the written documents, so that the people may not come out of the old and rusty routine, which flourished the superstitious trade of the uneducated priesthood. However the spirit of those great seekers of truth did not die and with the passage of time, the new generations of scientists, prevailed upon the existing rot and the clouds of the blind belief, were disappeared.

The torch bearers of the truth, however, had to face the brutal power which resulted in the sacrifices of their lives. The case in point is, Caparnicus, Brundo and Galalio, in series of sacrifices. They were sacrificed, when they encountered the blind faith of the existing bigotry and expressed, before the people, the discovery of the fact that 'Earth is round, and it revolves around the sun'. As the religious priesthood of those times did not want to assimilate this newly found truth in its impervious thought of universal existentialism.

The lowest rung, religious fundamentalists, are so shallow, in their knowledge of human-welfare, that they do not tolerate even the pious, pure and selfless services, rendered by the persons of other faiths, for the well fare of human beings in general without any consideration of cast and creed. The case in point is a recent macabre killing of an Australian Missionary 'Dr. Grahm Stewart Stens' alongwith his two teen aged sons in Orissa, (an occurrence on 24.1.99 night), who is believed to have worked for the last 30 years, for the free treatment to cure the leprosy patients in India. His only crime as read in the news papers was that he was a Christian and attended the work proposed by a body of some Christian Missionaries. Because of the power of his character and a radiance of his benevolence, some patients attended church and were attracted to Christianity, of which he was blamed to have been an instrumental being. Such an intensive uglification of civic behavior, was demonstrated in this incident, that no amount of condemnation and no words available in the dictionary can render even a tangential healing touch to this morbid abrasion of the human-consciousness which trembled, in desperation, when this missionary was burned alive alongwith his two teen aged sons, in the jeep itself, in which they were sleeping.

The political rivalries too, go eccentric many times and

adopt certain tracks, in which the rivals are hunted down and eliminated physically, through certain professionals, while so much topsy turvy, diplomatically, moded actions are initiated to divert the people's attention from the actual focus. Even in our society people do adopt certain means to get the interests of their rivals discarded and disposed off in a way that the other party would feel the pinch so much, that the flashes of intolerance would emerge out of the mind of the affected persons, which may become a cause of leaving a deep scar on the healthy environments in the locality, a village or a street. Such rivalry embedded in intolerance, would leave, your future generations too in quandary to face its consequential effects.

This abstract characteristic works as a reversal of the law of co-existence, amongst the nations even, which so many times has resulted in the wars and destructions of strong and civilised nations. The boundaries of the countries were changed, and the simmerings of disbelief's in different ideologies have engulfed, the different races in the dense clouds of mutual mistrust. Consequent upon which, the people/Government of so many countries remain under a constant threat of wars, thereby diverting all resources to develop military infrastructures on the cost of the developmental activities.

Actually the history books of the world right from the Roman Empire age to this modern space age, are full of wars and battles which took place to dominate the trade and commercial hubs of the civilized and fertile nations, were the results of this basic factor of intolerance towards the talented qualities of trade and developments of some races. The muscle power ruled the roost and took precedence on the delicate and subtle qualities of some refined races, which were zeroed, by the brute and physical power of assault and armoury.

There are still existing so many problem on the international planes, even now, which are attracting the world attention, through different international fora. Now the things have achieved such a pass, that the wise statesmanship and eloquence in oratory, is under stress to keep the clouds of war away, otherwise the whole civilization of the modern times may suffer a hard set back, in case this planet is entangled in

a. world war.

Despite religious and political intolerance. This demonic trait of human character is also finding slot in domestic behavior of all types of people. The presence of police posts, rush in the courts, big and posh buildings of practicing lawyers and the multiplication of the allied infrastructures, stand testimony to the fact, that 90% of the disputes and dispute-related cases, are the byproduct of the rivalries emanating from the intolerant attitudes of the people to justicious modes in the routine life. A lack of discriminatory sense for differentiating between bad and good, which mostly is the result of a dotted-line behavior of the individual to get one's selfish and avercial tendencies satisfied, become the store-house of all bitterness and indifference in the good relationship, in the cities and villages.

It is generally observed in the village society that mostly the disputes are related to envious derivations of the individual mind, which goes intolerant to some successful achievement of some of his progenic. This brand of dispute are found in the people who have a common base in the family tree. This is the result of narrow mindedness and a tunnel vision thinking. Mostly such unnecessary, and undesired torpic-in-phobe, mentality is possessed in uneducated people who simply go invidious after seeing that his progenic brother has found a slot, as a successful entrepreneur which would naturally make him a respectful person in society, as compared to him. He will go so absurd in his thought and action that his sentimental modules would remain under envious fire and tension within him, and naturally his pressure when released would create some wrong headed, auratic syndrome, which would colour the social environments with an uglification of the normal sorts. Such an exit of suppressed feelings may sometime catapult the whole balance, putting the family relations in utter disarray. This is where the venomous effects of the intolerance give an impetus to the posh bungalows of the lawyers and make the affected persons vulnerable to the exploits of the courts paraphernalias.

In all spheres of our activities, the most common factor are the ways and means which can be available for collecting more and more material wealth. The degree of fairness to achieve it, is not the worry of any body.

Even at our religious places, there are so many religious preachers and priests who do indulge in self-assertions and do not tolerate the plus points of others, rather they try to extract as much from the devotees pockets, as possible, even after passing some latent overtures against others, which explicitly points to the index of jealousy and intolerance being exercised by such people, whom the general devotee holds in high esteem. Such like tactics by the custodians of the faith, when a devotee coolly thinks with his balanced mind, his conscious comes under stress to peep through these translucent coverings of this multi layered camouflage of the priesthood. His judgment make him think and rethink over these simulating diatribes, which does not help to attract the people towards the faith, but may serve as a very good support system for ethiestic tendencies. So this sort of intolerance and obnoxious behavior towards the comradrie, puts the fair name of the religion in an utter jeopardy. The fall out of such practices naturally help in mush-rooming the more and more religious centres, to which the common man puts himself on his guards.

12

EVOLUTION OF CONSCIOUSNESS

The man would have been an incarnate of demonic and beastly nature, with only being called a creature with muscular strength, had there been no esteem. All the subtleness and sensitivities are the results of directions, which a person is destined to impart to its work-organs, because of the thinking modules, which the nature has provided to him. Actually the mental apparatus housed in the brain of a man by nature, makes him the supreme living being on earth. The degree and depth of his thinking power varies from man to man, as he is the only being in the universe, who can be trained and may acquire adaptations and co-ordinated movements in perpetual performances for doing so many jobs, which make him an integral part of the social system, who can generate wealth, through his physical and mental power.

However there being a difference in the grasp and previousness in one's cereberal subtleness, the intelligence level of each individual is also different. Hence the subtle blessings of nature as courage, initiatives, understanding bravery, boldness, decisiveness, efficiency, devotion, compassion, mercy, truthfulness, bliss etc. are also different in each person. Similarly the negative and degenerative traits in different persons are also of different degrees. This negativism has its bearings on the shallow intellectualism, which directs his energy channels to wrong-notions, and makes his consciousness devolve in arrogance and obstinacy, makes the person drab and dull, entangles him in a mesh of fear, ignorance, drudgery etc. there by creating a field of his auratic influences which limit his activism to animal instincts. The consciousness of such persons always works in subjugation to his lower mind, which degenerates his mentality to a mere self-acrimony and acerbity of temperament. The development of such persons do make them socially deciphered and delinquent.

The mental equilibrium of such persons however is subject to their environments and company of the people he is living with, and the social contours he is encountering. He may be reformed, refurbished and reoriented in his general behavior too. It has been experienced that some people who were consciously minions, were turned to be good citizens but there were some other, who turned to lawlessness and became problematic for healthy social environments, but the basic component was the degree of evolution of their consciousness.

Ours is a nation, which is touching to a colossal figure of 100 crores, when the world is knocking at the door of the twentieth-century. Out of which more than one-third, are living below the poverty line and the other about forty percent may be covered under lower middle and upper middle class standards. So about 73% of our population are at different level of evolvement of their consciousness. Untill and unless there remains a difference in this level, there would remain inequality and exploitation in our social fabric. These two basics, from which the human race yearns to be emancipated, may be having its dens in developed countries also, but their presence in the developing and under developed nations are felt more and more as the poor nations are having limited resources to create infrastructures to provide basic inputs to eradicate this menace. Hence the human resources development organisations are under constant pressure to meet with the aspirations of their people.

The exploitation of the people in different nations were the results of dissolution of the human consciousness, which remained in continuous abrasion to put a section of the society, from generation to generation under poverty and ignorance. No doubt the statesmanship of certain countries have worked hard to create infrastructures to ameliorate the lot of the exploited people. The form of Governance mostly being based on the democratic lines. The voice of people is now heard and no Government can be formed without the majority vote. Therefore the Governments in the offing have to plan the prospective developments of the exploited people the most. Hence this century has carried in its ambit the advancement of the people educationally, culturally, and ecologically. All these inputs have helped in the evolvement of consciousness of the depressed and downtrodden. Consequent upon all these steps, the scenario of the social developments have so changed, that gap between rich and poor have taken a reversal trend, economical, educationally and politically. The spirit of the poor is now being so evolved that even the poorest of poor have the possibility to get himself elected to manage the affairs of the country. In absolute terms, if we assume that each and every citizen get an opportunity to elevate himself. The twin dragons of inequality and exploitation may get a hard blow in getting its pace decelerated, and the emancipation of humanity as a whole can be speeded up. The drag on uncovering the thinking modules of the poor can be minimised perpetually; and they may get openings and initiatives which ultimately eliminate the sheepish and cowardly syndromes from their personal traits, thus the deluge of the sufferings and slavery die down and the exploited people come to understand the values of their esteem and inner consciousness.

The history is full of examples, where in the people who were from poor and unhealthy environments worked hard to elevate their consciousness and then went in direct clash with the ruling cliques to get their brothern freed from the yoke of slavery.

The evolved souls always do fructify an important feather in their cap, that is, the subtle quality of 'Self Respect'. These people sacrificed their lives to maintain their self respect. We had several heroes, who embodied in them the strongest and burning desires and their morality stood like a rock to the cruel ways of the rulers. On political level Maharana Partap a Rajput chieftain is stated to have remained hungry alongwith his family in the jungles, but did not allow the self respect of the nation to be muzzled down. Similarly in recent past too our national heroes as gadri-babas, S. Sewa Singh thekriwala, accepted the challenges of the brute power of states and resisted their on slaughts on their body frames.

On religious front too, the history of Sikh Gurus and Sikh warriors, do tell the tales of valour and sacrifices. who did not compromise on their self respect, even if they were put to brute and cruel ways of torchers, before they left their mortal frames. They were the shining stars on our horizons and possessed elevated souls, who were very very near to the bliss absolute, even when they were being crucified.

The evolved souls have such deep carvings on our culture that the international thought takes it as a great deterrent, to think twice while undertaking some sort of adventurism against such nations. Actually this is the spirit of sacrifice which make the nations evolve consciously. This is the stare, into the eyes of others, which make the whole scenes clearer to the exploiters, attackers, looters, rioters, perpetrators etc. to judge as to, of what metal the rival race is made of. Even your enemy would bow to you, if you go down in the battle field fighting, for your cause. There are certain examples in history, that even the conqueror had a feel in his esteem that his rival was a brave person. Such is the evaluation of the evolved consciousness.

During the British rule, our destiny was guided by the English, who created such controls and commands that our people were covered under the deluge of ignorance. No educational facilities, no opening for career's, were available for our nationals whatever we produced through our sweat and hard labour were carted to their own native land. The result being that the soul of our nation remained confined and our general public remained under a tunnel vision. We were encouraged to practice upper and lower casts syndromes untill and unless certain persons of our country with elevated souls, came forward to get our ignorant and uneducated people awakened from their sleeping and sluggish attitudes and made them aware of their rights, although they themselves burned their calories in the dark cells of jails.

In nut shell this is only the awareness and awakened self-esteem, which inspires a spirit in nations, without which a nation cannot remain a nation and a race has got no meaning at all.

With the change of times now, the imprints of elevated consciousness and covetous previousness of our national mind, had been camouflaged with so many question marks, on our future cetidals which have now come under the control of avericial and greedy leadership. As all the cybernetics of our prospective developments, and all the struts and columns which are supporting our system to eliviate our people from drudgery and ignorance, to boost up the spirit and esteem of the Indian mind, have now come under pressure and are exposed to rust and cracks, by the so called leaders, whose patriotism has now mostly become a salable commodity, impregnated with diplomatic jugglery and a rank hypocracy. The common man is totally confused in the populous slogans of opportune politics which is taking the people to degeneration and denigration from the real focus.

There was a time, when our leaders with their evolved and elevated spirit, worked over the dotted line realism and gave a clear cut and direct message to our people, that there is no runners up in the game of patriotism. Always it would be a victory or a defeat. No medieval stage at all. But the modern pseudo prudence of our helmsmen do adorn the winning postures even on defeat, after putting in certain 'if' and 'buts' under which they cover up their own negativism, thus spreading a confusing mesh for the general public. They would place their arguments before the people, that there defeat is a victory of certain fundamentals. Thus they put the voice of the electorate to abuse and absurdity. No body would ever think of principles and parameters of refineness, for which our patriots of yester-years have suffered and even sacrificed their lives. How the credibility of the politics is being degenerated? who cares?

Such invectuous overtures by our politicians are adopted when their own averice interlaced with felonious intent, is put before the people, and the person concerned comes under the flabergast probes of the common man. This trend has been adopted by all and sundry, who-so-ever comes under the detective eyes of the law. What degree of contamination he has created to the health of the system, is not his concern rather he would incorporate all his gimmickry acrobats to justify his faults. The general public not being so acquainted with all such catapults of politics would most often submit to the dictates of pollution displayed by such people. However the damage assimilated in the body politik, takes its slot, thus the cumulative affects of such endeavors by our politician put the whole fabric to a sustained stink. So the self service these days has polluted the evolved consciousness of the nation as a whole, to which the common man does not take exception and goes on flowing with the tide, however unhealthy or suffocating it may become.

13

COMMERCIAL EXPLOITS

The world now has come under an utter ridicule of satellite reflections through different channels which are being, visualised by the people through out the world. The flabergast attitudes of the people of different nations are naturally attracted towards the small screens, so as to know the cultural-gaps, which cover the modern marketing trends, the sensual modes, the architectural and aesthetic senses, the geographic layouts. the modes of travelling, the navigational sophystories the technological advances, the space explorations, the political exploitations, the modern war techniques, the tactical modes of terrorism and the new initiatives in space explorations etc.

If we leave aside the people of developed countries, whose intellectual communicative modes do comparatively stand higher in the pervasiveness and practices of all the modern basics, other people, belonging to developing and under developed countries, are mostly come under the exploits of the modern, trends, displayed by the small screen. As the majority of the population of such countries, do fall a prey to the glamour and sensual advertisements of the small screen, which depicts mostly the western style of living, optimised and oriented in a way which is much more away from the reality and rationals of the actualism of under developed world. But these sections of the people in poor nations do come under a deluge of hypnotism and hypocracy and try to feel satisfaction to assimilate these displays as a real life. They want to incorporate all these apparents and impiricals in their practical lives. Only a microscopic number of persons, who are destined to have regulated their mental digestion, through the sublimation of their personal experiences, do understand the rationals and rhythms of such phobiatic isometricism in practical derivations of routine life, while the rest are carried away by the glamourous overtones of daily displayed commercial exploits, which do try to detest the realism of this cosmetic coruscates of the dazzling men and women, well parloured to delude and deceit the watching eyes.

So the people who are slated at the lower rungs of their minds, are the slaves to their senses, do try to follow the dictates of the small-screen-shows, and opt even the questionable means to reach to' that illusion, which lands them to degeneration and disgrace within the limits of their own culture. Apparently the net gain is only the pollution of one's character and a droop of ones self-respect.

Actually I am saying it a degeneration and pollution with reference to our Indian values or to the values of certain nations with even more conservative societies. As far as the western culture is concerned, which is dominantly displayed, in almost all the channels, naturally, leaves its imprints on the cultural fields of the conservative societies of the poor nations, which is a contravention on their values, as a result, there have appeared so many ruptures in the original patterns of their systems. The original thought of such nations feels odd to walk on this alien spectrum of societical chess. The conservative tandems of the orthodoxy are under an extra pressure to legislate new laws, to keep their flock in desired parameters, who are attracted to western way of life, which imbibe in its ambit more freedom, more body exposures, more hi-fi orientations in their routine life.

In certain countries which are more under the influences of religious bigotry and fundamentalism, which resist vehemently any type of dent in their old values are forced to issue edicts, to contain their younger generation in their orthodox beliefs. Still the influences of commercial exploits of western culture do spill over all types of bonds and boundaries, and make their magnanimity show, in the deep recesses of their mind-set.

The propinquity of human mind is always affected by the appeasing orientations, which affect the younger people the most, as the adolescent stage in particular has a good amount of cushion to absorb and assimilate the sensual attributes, to which the young blood finds itself fantasized. The wisdom gained through experience is not still the subject of their minds. So the images left by the commercial advertisements on the new generation are taken as objectionable and pungent, by the social scientists of conservative societies.

The glamour and exposure of bodies may be an asset of the western culture, but the same is considered immoral and injurious in our societies and also in many other nations, which are even more conservative as compared to us.

The females of the west are quite advanced and complex free and avail all available opportunities to work shoulder to shoulder with their men folk in all fields. No field is now alien to the western women. Even they do not bind themselves as an apron to the men, after matrimony or marriages, rather they exercise their own free will, as per their intelligence and wisdom, and are at liberty to break the wed lock, if the marriage partners are lacking in understanding, goodwill and can not walk on the same wave length. Of course their laws also stand as a safeguard to their system.

But the problem with our people is that they mostly immitate them in sensuoul syndromes only. However our younger generation, the young girls particularly are also coming up in all fields at par with our men, and we are finding some young girls have taken to field of Army, Airforce, Police etc. which were considered as the men dominated professions only. This contiguity of the western culture has shown some positiveness in our younger women too, which is appreciable.

It is quite obvious therefore that some initiative and adventurism have received a push from the western culture and our younger generation too have a tempering and tuning to follow the advances of scientific and technological developments, but the trend of a 'blinded-eyed-flock-gait' without applying any intelligence denominations, is injurious to the health of our own culture. The majestics of piousness and purity which have assimilated in our character, when receive an accentrics of push and pressure, to deviate from morals and ethics of your own way of life, the whole balance is disturbed and your social fabric comes under unnecessary strains and your own values get polluted.

One more aspect of the commercial exploitation, is the modern days techniques of terrorism, kidnapping exhortions, burglaries, narcotics etc., which are displayed in fine tuned graphics and under well versed directions, which normally stem in short-cuts to richness and material wealth. It does induce and inspire the younger generation to opt for such practices within the same parameters, which actually lead the unmatured minds to wrong paths. The displays of such exploits on screen are totally devoid of the practicability and actualism which simply land the adopters of such practices to destruction and desperation. The adolescence can not fore see the hollowness of such ados and they get their own lives spoiled and the environments around polluted.

We read in newpapers and also see on T.V. screens that certain youngsters, when caught by the law enforcing agencies, and are interviewed on the screen, admitting that how they were got entangled in this criminal net, of murder, loot or narcotics. The main factor they say was an inspiration, they received from the criminal exploits on the cinema or small screen. Any thing devoid of intelligence and wisdom would pollute the system as a whole and land these short-cuts followers to a tailored made mesh of crime, in which the crime bird would flutter its wings sooner or later.

In addition to the glamour and crime prone displays in the commercial exploits, there is a camouflage of confusing and unidirectional advertisements for promoting marketing of consumer goods of certain trading houses. Which are changing everyday with the new names and epithets, backed up by glamourous ladies or handsomely built bolly-wood personalities or certain persons of substance, which have created so much confusion that a person of ordinary prudence comes under their exploits. From ordinary broom to clean the floor of the house, brands of soaps, tooth paste, brushes, cookwares, electronic appliances, medicines, health prone-devices, with attractive scenes in the backdrop, have put the purchasing power of the ordinary household, out of gear, but have given an impetus to extravagance to those who do indulge in lavish spending. Both the categories are tempted to the modern market techniques being advertised by the small screen. The consequential effects are, the stuffing of house-hold-shelves and kitchen cabinets. Which become breeding spots for insects and cockroaches. Thus the environmental pollution also creeps in.

Judging the whole spectrum, with a graded intelligence and in a rational way, it stands to reason that the man would have a balance of mind only, if he remains in himself. Any apparent or adopted biorhythms, would lead to a speculative philosophy, which will keep you away from knowledge and truth. Only your own mother will yearn for your welfare and progress, an alien would always be in bargaining attires. Swami Viveka Nand Ji, a piller of our culture and philosophy says "Every body should take up his own ideal and endeavor to accomplish it. That is a sure way to progressing, than take up other men's ideals, which he can never hope to accomplish".

I do not hesitate to admit that every young man, aspires for new adventures, new explorations, to know the reality. This is good to the extent, which may make you discover certain existing, but, hidden facts, but to be crazy and blind followers of sensual attributes in pursuance of commercial exploits, do speak of lolly-pop or a gheto-culture only. (I am writing this as I have also gone through this in my young age, as my mind too was very much indulgent to such attributes. Actually what I am saying at the end of my 68 years on this planet, were also my choicest hi-cups at the prime time when the wall clock of my age was substracting its tick-tick, from the calculus of my own life).

I do take this opportunity to clarify that the craze for sensual desire, works more or less on the same graphics. It may be solenoided through commercial advertisements, which is termed as a lolly-pop culture or may have been catalysed, through gheto-culture as were the conditions in fifties, but the level of fantasism in the young minds, is more or less the same. An unmatured mind is always emotional and crazy as it tries to catch up his own shadow.

The mirage is illusion and illusion is mirage which never do exist, which does not exist, cannot he reached. So try, to be in your real-self. Always try to see the soul of your motherland in the poor and needy who are the roots of our inspiration and strength. Never become a slave to alien sparkles, which would only pollute your minds. Watch and observe, to acquire knowledge, if you can. Try to improve your mental constitution not the pollution of your character.

14

POPULATION AND POLLUTION

One does not need any combinations or complex reckonings to rely on a belief that the world as a whole is under great pressure to keep the essentials of sustenance of all kinds of existence, in a perfect balance, ecologically, and environmentally. The root cause of all types of maladies and malaise, is the population blast in all over the world. The population of developing and under developed countries are bursting to its seams now and hence their people are, facing all types of pollution in their environments, which also do reflect on the domains of others.

According to one estimate, the fertility rate of the under developed countries are more than six per woman, while that of the developed countries, it is in-between 1.6 to 2.0. It is quite obvious that the poor nation will remain polluted and infested in all types of diseases. A justicious thinking would give you an undoubtable understanding that whatever aid the world organisation may provide to such nations, their conditions would not be visibly improved, untill and unless they themselves have a governance which may create infrastructures to ameliorate their conditions. The priority, of course, would go to put a stop to the growing population.

Out of the 192 nations, only 67 are such who have the fertility rate at par with or below, their replacement level. Rest of the 125, are adding to polluting this planet in all spheres, i.e.

physical environmental and ecological etc.

I may be permitted to assess the prospective and projections of my own country. According to national graphic society, "The Indian population at the time of independence, that is, in 1947, was 350 millions people. Fifty years later, it is about to reach 1 billion. Though India was the 1st country to adopt a family planning policy and has slowed down its growth rate, it is still projected to become world most populous country by 2050". The projections are apparently true, as when we are at the door steps of 21st century now, our population has touched to plus 99 crores and 75 lacs. With this very rate our population density would increase by three folds, in the next fifty years. The struts of our infrastructures would buckle down under the pressure of galloping necessities, which all persons in this age of space would aspire for.

Moreover the fertility rate of under developed world, which in some countries is above 7, per woman now, would change the whole world to sighs and tears, as the pitch of the existencial planes would be so queered with the twists and turns of the circumstances, that even an utter chaos may not be a suitable word for the uglification of the environments.

The man's journey from the Roman Empire to present space age is full of adventures which have worked its way in arduous and trying conditions, to make human life more platable and worth living. It has taken the developmental perspectives in agricultural, medical, irrigational, technological and space explorations, to its logical level. In perpetual and continued process, the man has now taken to the exploration of the new planets, with respect to its, textures, climates, environments etc. to know as to whether some process could be initiated, to make any of the planet, prohumanist, to live on or not. Because the conditions which are being created on the earth itself are putting the capabilities of the man's intellectualism to an intolerable stresses, in working out more possibilities and probabilities to save this planet from utter jeopardy to live on.

No doubt that world is growing larger and less equal. There are a few countries with smaller families which are shrinking in population. Also there is a difference in urbanisation level amongst developing and developed nations, but the growth rate in under developed countries is so intense in magnitudes that the global pressure on development apparatus, is recording an incessant increase. It is quite obvious that the countries with shrinking population have developed an inbuilt apparatus, which are monitoring the educational core under which the conceptual constitution of the mental attitudes of their people are getting a tuned synchronism with the pace of modern age. Their main criteria is to see, that the life of each individual citizen is valuable while keeping their fertility rate down, they have also stretched the lives of their people to longevity. They have planned their schemes to be pro-people and pollution free that is why their people are well off and enjoy even their path-way-facilities, without any strain on their minds. All their citizens are fully satisfied for the three basic essentials of life, that is home, hearth and helmet.

Contrary to this, the countries with more fertility rate like Nigeria, Zaire and so many others are adding enermously to the population growth on the globe. People all over the world are now understanding the dangers of, our out stripped population, but how many people would be too many? are still proving illusive. Middle range estimates of the planet's carrying capacity according to one estimate runs between 7.7 billions to 12 billions, which number we will enter in the next 50 years. After which even the green revolution which is multiplying the food articles since approximately by three decades, through its scientific researches, may also begin depleting.

If the entire world consumed its resources profligately, what would be the future of the man kind is anybody's guess there should be no illusion on this issue. We are already pushing ourselves against some apparent limits, when the planet is being loaded with approximately 80 million people every year.

The most pertinent question which rises in our minds now is, the under developed countries which are already full to their brim are fmding it very very difficult to feed their people. We actually watch their citizens, living in tethered straw huts, with naked bodies, having the body profiles as a bundle of bony structures, with a cover of shabby and shorn out skin.

Their children being surrounded by the mosquitoes and flies. Their helmets being surrounded by patches of dirt and stinking water pools. They eat only some jungle vegetation as food. Their bulged out eye-balls, mal-nutritioned bodies, with no infrastructural facilities what-so-ever, speak of their ugly environments, which have put them under a deluge of multi-dimensional pollution. The mothers are seen taking their mal-nutritioned babies, in their laps, who try to suck her breast, which deludes the baby who tries to extract milk, but it proves to be deceptive and a vain hope of the innocent soul.

Regarding the mental or political pollution the poor people of under developed world, are not more conscious about, as they have to get themselves, recovered from their basic needs first, which are their very basic ingredients to live. The ratio of the developed and under developed peoples are approximately 1:4, that means, that as per the projections of 7 billion of total population, approximately $7 \times 4/5 = 5.6$ billions are supposed to fall under the mal-nutritioned category. There may be some variation in these figures, as the scientists of the world are busy in exercising all options to get the human beings emancipated from sufferings, but the number of sufferers being mind boggling, no apparent visible effects are coming on record.

We should also be clear in our mind, that when our neighbour is facing all the complexities of pollution and suffocations, its effects would also spill over to our own house. This very factor is applicable in our global dealings as well. This factor also leads the people of poor countries to find certain pastures in other lands, which gives a boost to their discretionary thought to work as migrant labourers in foreign lands. According the statistics of year 1990, about 2% of the world population lives outside the country of their birth, for which the vital factor is the economic conditions, although they are not met with open arms by the original inhabitants, as they carry with them their cultural habits and mental attitudes, to which the host country takes as a major impediment to their pure environments.

The main profession of the migrants, are a help in domestic and industrial fields, but they are generally treated shabbily and with discrimination by the original citizens, as a result both remain under stress and create a field for mental pollution. In about last 30 years, the oil rich middle east countries, have attracted most of the work force from the Asian countries. This tempo of migratory pressures are likely to increase in the following decades, as the industrialised world native-labour-pool, is projected to shrink, while the developing world work force is increasing by geometric progression. This spill over of population naturally carry alongwith, their inheritance of living conditions as well as the trivial of the cultural infections to which the local people do not at all welcome.

Where the life expectancy has shown an exhorbitant increase, all over this planet, the pressure on infrastructural constitution and per capita increase in energy consumption have also increased, which is a direct index of the people's advancement.

But as stated above, that 4 people out of 5, are causing a spread in the pollution of environments. It therefore stands to reason that if the undeveloped nations, do not take the bull of fertility rate by the horns, this planet would be enmeshed in suffocation. What catastrophic developments may usher in, is any body's guess? So the philosophers, the planners, the religious organisation all owe a responsibility to think and rethink. They should come out from the old and rusty doctrines and dogmas, to save the mankind from further stink. Otherwise if the existence does not exist, what the remanents of the 21st century would say to the incumbents of the 20th century?

I am just a minion and do not have the wisdom to give any advice to the enlightened organisers and planning managers of our country, or for that purpose even the planners of international projects, but I may extend my humble opinion as per my own mental level, as to how I do see the explosion of population blast over this planet.

From the above discussion, it is precisely clear that our planet would adopt a shape of behive for living cells, in the next 50 years and there would be no space remaining, to accommodate any further populace.

The question now confronting the intelligentsia is, to find ways and means, under which each individual may be made conscious to grapple with this menace, so that this planet may be saved from further uglification. This mainly is the subject of understanding the vagaries and adversities, of this unprecedented load, which is the root cause of all problems, confronting the human race in whole world. It is quite obvious that an awareness and a tinker in the minds of lowly placed and uneducated persons of the underdeveloped nations, to kindle a spark in their insight regarding uncontrolled increase in population, are the most challenging task of the day. Otherwise the process is in the offing, which may cause total destructions of various social orders, which may put an extra burden on the future demographers.

The religious organisations and religious preachers, can play a positive role to get the general public bring, on the right path, to respond fully to the scheme of family planning. Ignoring the dangers of this unbridled sensual desires any further, would be suicidal for the world as a whole.

All persons on the earth are basically divine and have an aptitude to hear the voice of one's consciousness provided the dogmatic beliefs are not given an unnecessary boost by certain religious preachers. Nothing would exist, if there remains nothing, and the explosion in population takes this planet to nothingness. Every right thinking person or organisation, should see reason and convey a message of diligence and wisdom, which should be correlated to existence and survival. Simple preaching of doctrines and dogmas, of one's creed without intelligence or covetousness, would lead to rejection of the present time imperatives. Its effects may become a cause of decimation of the whole civilization.

We are standing at such a cross, that there is no scope of looking back, but to act swiftly with a courage of conviction, to control the rising curves of population graphs. The old frame of 20th century is already spreading its weak and withered look over the paths on which the man has treaded during the last millennium. The beseeching old look are now reverently assessing our past unresponsive attitudes which limited the man's actualism only to the sensual and lustful desires which consequently kept on loading this planet with sustained effects of pollution on every bit of life-prone existence.

15

LAST LAUGH OF THE CENTURY

The span of time from 1000 A.D. to 2000 A.D. (1999 A.D.) has covered in its ambit the various phases of human evolutions, which have been compartmentalised by Historian as below:

(i) The Middle age,

(ii) The discovery age,

(iii) The Industrial age, and

(iv) The space age.

The eras of different ages have galvanised the conception and practices, as per the imperatives of the times nomenclatured as a recognition of politically achieved, features in a particular field. This was the result of scribbles and strains on the mental modules to discover the hidden truth, through the scientific endeavours of the man, who has been exploring the different modes to discover new trade routs and areas, the new innovations in engineering and technology, the new adventures to explore the other planets etc.

My scope of discussion in this chapter relates only to 20th century, hence I will be limiting my conceptual curvatures to this time-slot. No doubt the successes achieved by this century was a continued process, to which credit also goes to the scientists and technologists of the previous century, but I would discuss only the net positive ends, achieved in the last hundred years.

The 20th century persons of substance, that is the scientists, technologists, sailors, soldiers, explorers Adventurists, mystics, monks, patriots, politicians, architects, and engineers etc. have recorded their positive achievements right from the early years to mid sixties of this time slot, which have recorded a steep optimised level, and are still in the process of development, when this slot is on the verge of phasing out.

The earliest recorded technological feat was the '1st' prototype flight of motor-powered air-plane, by Wright brothers in the year 1903 which was subsequently well punctuated by various electronics, feats of T.V./computers from time to time, upto the man's walk on the moon, which closes with the galactic images from hubble space telescope and new exploration of Jupiter and Mars. All the above technological developments are for the benefit of the humanity as a whole. However I record my suspected monovalent thought for the achievement of Einstein's special theory of relativity in 1905, which contributed to revelation of quantum physics, explaining the behavior of atoms, because it became a major cause to destroy the human civilization during the world war second (Discussed in this chapter on a later page). Even now the civilization stands on the brink of destruction as the nuclear dangers have adopted draconian dimensions. Thus such an invention which if not used prudently may destroy the whole existence.

The beginning of the century was a period, when the control and commands of Governance of different nations were with the mighty military powers. But the people's minds were coloured in mysticism, the guides or mystics were generally puritan's, and an aura of their waves made the environments also pure simple and serene. Although the social contours were punctuated with the cult of feudalism, rich and poor gap, inequality and exploitation and brute state powers, which were the stinking irritants, the people had to confront. Religiously the people were God fearing, and full of compassion, generosity and were sociable. The Hindu monks, Muslim Sufi, Faqirs and the Sikh missionaries were the embodiments of subjectivity which guided and influenced the Indian sub-continent to be mentally pure and pious, serene and sedate, sociable and helpful, although the disputes amongst rich and poor, feudal lords and simple peasants were existing.

We the Indians were ruled by the British, who treated our people as their subjects and used them to the interest of their own nation. They have spread a camouflaged mesh, on our social environs, which promoted a syndrome of slavery and serfdom in the mind set of our simple and uneducated population. The enlighted and subjective esteem of our leaders have gone through the game and gimmicks of the Empire custodians and they had given a clarion call to awaken the Indian consciousness through different organisations, which set different modes of struggle to liberate our people from bondage of slavery, the cybernetics of the Empire had already come under strain and the Government machinery had been kept on their tenter hooks, by the collective wisdom of Indian leaderships, from all directions, which pointed their fingers to Delhi throne. The leaders which emerged from the smell and smears of our mother land, were men of integrity, stood for honest and simple livings. Their practical lives were truthful spiritually, and temporal politically. They were the walking morals on earth, who influenced and guided the people to positive traits of human characters. There were no pollution in the minds of those people, no averice, no hypocracy, no simulation. They were precise in percept and practice. Hence the general public held them in high esteem. It was the conviction of their character that even the simple and uneducated people got their consciousness kindled to the extent that they could face the brute power of the Empire without fear. The massacre of Jalianwala Bagh was a case, when the people of all casts and creeds, sacrificed their lives, without any cavil and carp. The selfless services of the leaders towards their people, inspired the general public to bear the brunt of the power of Empire.

Also this century has experienced two world wars in which the military powers of various blocks were put to test. These wars were fought in the second and fifth decades of the century. The 1st war was fought by conventional weapons while the second was a total holocaust when the destruction power of the newly introduced nuclear bomb was demonstrated in two cities of Japan, in which the people died in thousands and lacs were rendered maimed and seriously injured.

According to one account published in newspaper Hindu, on 7.8.98, under the title head:

"HIROSHIMA WAS WIPED OUT IN 10 SECONDS"

(It was given with reference to a Japanese documentary as under:

"The 'little boy' atomic bomb that obliterated Hiroshima, released lethal dose of radiation, with in one millionth of a second.

The radiation fell on people, even before they saw the flash — —— the uranium 235 bomb exploded 567 meters above the city at' 8-15 a.m. (23-15 GMT) on August 6, 1945, after being released by the US B-29 bomber Enola Gay.

In the following three seconds, a flash appeared, heralding a fire-ball, that moved fast than the speed of sound, the documentary showed in a computer graphic simulation.

Within 10 second of the detonation, the shock wave wiped out every thing within 4 kms, blowing away homes, twisting iron frames and throwing bodies into the air.

About 1,40,000 people died by the end of 1945)".

This hollocaust had left a sustained effect of genetic imbalances, which made the would be mothers, give birth to deformed and deranged babies. This was the blemish of science, which proved to have played an obnoxious role towards humanity and civilization. The injurious effects of this catastrophy are still showing their scars on the spine of the passing out century's old body frame.

After stoppage of war, the soul of the planet was stirred, with a cynical syndrome emanating from the wisdom and sublimed subtleness of refined thinking of the statesmanship, which stood aghast, devoid of all aesthetics of the civil responsibility. Finally this misdirection of the scientific power by the military strategists, was taken as a crime towards humanity by the world leaders. The wise counsels derived an abstract conclusions, to create certain commands and controls to bridle any misadventure in future. The outcome was the creation of united nation, organisation (U.N.O.) which is now looking after the affairs of political war-prone disputes.

The subsequent most important event of the Indian subcontinent was the independence of India, on August 15, 1947 while the country was also partitioned as two independent nations. Pakistan was carved out of India, which was mainly based on the concept of Islamic religion. This division was marked with catastrophic developments, engineered by the fundamentalists on both sides of the dividing line. Communal riots were erupted and thousands of people had to leave their homes and hearths. There was a carnage of murders, rapes, loot, fire for which mainly the innocent people on both sides were targetted by the rival religious bigotry. The women and young girls, on both sides were dragged and forced to submission and bore the ugliest forms of masculineous barbarism. So severe and brute were the torcherous techniques used by the protagonists of rival fundamentalists for butchery and murders that sanity and wisdom was totally mowed down. It was the worst form of uncivilised and barbaric behavior, where every body demonstrated their muscle power, to the lowest level of the whims of ones individual mind, which outmaneuvered the brute and barbaric dynamics displayed by others in the long past. As such it was a holocaust where in the sanity stood aghast and sweated, under the shock of societical infarcation. Even the demonic and draconian mind-sets of the previous, barbarity exercised by the cruelest of the cruel stood defeated. For about one month, it was free for all as the law and order was lost in vacuum. So to say the law enforcing agencies on both sides, were over worked and were lost in flux, without any direction from the respective Governments what-so-ever. Those were the darkest days in the history of sub-continent which I had the chance to observe in my childhood days.

After this great upheaval, under which the ousted people on both sides, found some breathing space in the form of refugees, the Government sponsored relief measures were undertaken, and by and by, the law and order agencies emerged to show their writ. The rehabilitation work was speeded up to settle the ousted people in their new homes, which were left behind the people of other community. Everything turned topsy-turvy. The refugees found only half burnt and demolished katcha helmets or houses which could not give them any protection without repairs.

The legacy of this barbarity interlaced in fundamentalism are still playing a hide and seek in this subcontinent. It is a very very long subject but here it has been discussed only briefly which was important for my subject, in the context of this event, which was an important mile stone of this century.

Despite this event, this slot of time, has also canopied people's war in China, division of Berlin by constructing a bricked wall, and also the demolition of the same after about four decades. Creation of power blocks, that is, the socialist block and capitalist block, after which an era of cold war remained a special feature on the global politics. There were so many skirmishes and political acrobats which were supported and catalysed by the two power blocks. Finally the will of the people prevailed and the socialist block crumbled under the weight of their own ill-conceived ideology of pseudo-socialism, under one party rule. This type of Governance which is legalised by suppressing the popular will of the people, do sustain cracks in their struts, no sooner its ideologues or promoters vanish away with the tides of times, and people are permitted to give vent to their feelings. These were the main features which influenced the world history in its perspective.

The second important point is the advent of space-age-era, based on the technological and scientific advancements. The most vital scientific achievement was capping a soviet U.S. space race, which resulted in a walk on the moon by an American Austronat named Neil Armstrong in 1969. The subsequent exploration for Jupiter and Mars are still going on in a perpetual development potentials of science and technology.

In India too, some positive achievements have been made in the satellite-orbiting, and rocketry trajections, according to the imperatives of the space science. Only recently Indian scientific cetidals have proved their competency and comprehension on the use of nuclear energy which was also followed by Pakistan Government.

Now I would take this discussion which would deal with the modern trends, on which the mental constitution of our helmsmen, are being directed. The most of the politicians these days are polluting the multifaceted environments on political and societical plans. This has taken a global orientations.

The generation of more wealth, through trade and commerce, based on the scientific advances on the global level, have given an impetus to the money channels for advancement of the civilization. Obviously the custodians of the laws of the lands too, have got their discretionary spending level, fairly raised up, which have created new modules in the individual characteristics of modern politicians. Most of these people have developed a craze for averice and greed. This ultimately has led to the decomposition and degeneration of the human values.

The man these days may go to any extent to collect more and more material wealth. The second generation political masters who rule the roost now, on different levels of political spectrum, have put the name and fame of their founders to an utter degradation. The integrity and credibility of most of modern leaders are the first causality in refineness of thought and principled activism. All types of gimmicks and gimcracks are used to duck and interpolate the illegal wealth and material gains, through misuse of authority. Of late, that is, after seventh decade of the century, the scandles and scams have rocked the roots of our Governing basics, and most of the time is wasted in investigations and debating such issues in parliament and legislative assemblies. The hard earned money of the people, who are the so called masters of the politicians (as modern politicians simulate) is being pocketed by these so called servants of the people. But when the detective hands catch hold of them, they use all available knickknacks and flimsy trumperies to defend themselves. They are proving themselves so much drooped, that even after getting exposed on the documentary proofs, they would not leave the chair, and if at all the circumstances so warrant they would try to negotiate the terms in such a way that the seat of authority may remain their own fiefdom as original.

Gone are the days, when men like Sh. Lal Bahadur Ji

Shastri, our ex-premier, while working as a railway minister in the ministry of Pt. Jawahar Lal Nehru took the responsibility of a railway accident on his own shoulders and resigned his seat immediately, although so many people tried to convince him, that it was not his fault. He did not oblige those people and did not compromise his principled stand, that, all successes of the department would go to the officialdom while any failure would be his responsibility. He maintained this line of action through out his life.

Unlike the new breed of politicians, who are not willing to owe any responsibility for their own misdeeds, even if their misdemeanors are appearing as the 1st head line of newspapers. So much is the decline in the performance curves of our political leader's present graphics are that the voice of the people is lost in drudgery and nothingness. All geometrics are now centered to grab power, by hook or by crook, hypocracy or hybridation, square or circular orientations, by heckling or harrassing etc. except principled politics. To stick to chair has become a bane of reckoning these days. This trend has not only polluted their own minds, rather the whole society has now come under the stink of greed and averice.

The stink is also penetrating into the public mind in general, who too are getting their mind-sets topoed, like that of their political masters. The discrimination and compassion, is totally vanishing, rather the selfishness and personal interest are taking credence on everything. Not only the people's minds are getting polluted even the physical, environmental, and social aptitudes are contributing to the ugliness of the respective regions. The voice of sanity is vanishing.

No doubt, there have appeared, sky-rocketing towers and building, snakewaved-multistoreyed bridges and roads, the underground metros and undersea water ways, which shows that technology of this century have covered mariculous potentialities. Even the international skies these days, are born with planes which are without thunder and without any microwaves, to be detectable by the refinely tuned new generation radars. But still the people are burning, as it is only the level of one's consciousness, which can give you calmness and peace of mind, as never the man can get a bliss absolute by the power and pelf, titles or titans money or materials. It is only the balance of mind, pure and pious thought, rhythmic civic behavior, selfless service aptitudes, which can make the character and esteem of a nation strong and subtle. It is the dire need of the next century so that future of mankind may remain safe.

My country men your substantials are being watched by the world today. The electronics medias have put you on transparent isometrics your own conscious is always watching you. See reason and shed all sorts of complexes, do not try to deceive your own people your own mother land and the soul of the planet as a whole. If character is lost, nothing is left, see the writings on the walls the next century may not tolerate your flimsy-trumperies.

INDEX